To

With wishes of peace.

DIVALDO FRANCO
BY THE SPIRIT
JOANNA DE ÂNGELIS

GLORIOUS DAYS

Authorized edition by Centro Espírita Caminho da Redenção.
Salvador (BA) – Brazil

Miami
1st ed. 2020

ISBN 978-1-947179-68-4

Original title in Portuguese:
Dias Gloriosos
(Brazil, 2018)

Translated by: Claudia Dealmeida

Revised by: Ily Reis

Cover design by: Cláudio Urpia

Editorial Supervision by: Lívia Maria Costa Souza

Layout by: Rones Lima – instagram.com/bookebooks_designer

Edition of
LEAL PUBLISHER
8425 Biscayne Boulevard, Ste. 104
Miami, FL 33138
www.lealpublisher.com
Phone: (305) 206-6447

Authorized edition by Centro Espírita Caminho da Redenção – Salvador (BA) – Brazil

INTERNATIONAL DATA FOR CATALOGING IN PUBLICATION (ICP)

F895   FRANCO, Divaldo.

FRANCO, Divaldo Pereira (1927) Glorious Days 1st. ed. / authored by the Spirit Author Joanna de Ângelis [psychographed by] Divaldo Pereira Franco. Translated by Claudia Dealmeida; revised by Ily Reis - Miami (FL), USA: Leal Publisher, 2020.

192 p.; 21cm

Original title: *Dias Gloriosos*

ISBN: 978-1-947179-68-4

1. Spiritism 2. Atualidade. 3. Moral. I Franco, Divaldo Pereira, 1927 – II. Title.

CDD 133.9
CDD 133.7

CONTENTS

GLORIOUS DAYS

*U*nremitting scientific discoveries and technological advances open the way to new and fascinating perspectives on life in general, and on individuals in particular.

The horizon of human thought progressively broadens to reach unfamiliar heights.

Culture and the arts bring us sweeping visions of the possibilities that modern development can make available to almost everyone.

Fertile imaginations come up with exceptional resources for human growth and progress in the different areas of knowledge and experience.

With distances around the world markedly shortened, humans slowly set out to conquer planets closer to the earth. As it was once the case with the moon, it is now with Mars.

Information Technology enables easy and convenient access to all sorts of information at almost the speed of thought.

From the privacy of our own homes, we can practically travel the entire world, establish instant connections and find everything we want due to the valuable resources of online communication.

Computer-assisted microsurgery reduces the risk of death. Surgical procedures and therapeutic processes prolong the physical existence of the patients who can afford them. New techniques change medical protocols and old pharmaceutical formulations. However, this barrage of breakthroughs is not limited to this area alone. It takes place across every known field of study as it endeavors to keep pace with the incidence of modern advances.

Despite these invaluable achievements that so enhance the world, however, the cruel and menacing monster of war remains a presence at the borders, claiming innumerable lives. Hunger continues to besiege hundreds of millions of men, women, and children that wither away far from any show of mercy or compassion, entirely forgotten by the socalled civilized nations. The ugly face of crime –in all its perversity– swells up and devours the most beautiful blooms of hope, causing widespread fear even among those living in high-security fortresses. Vice runs rampant. Substance dependence, smoking and sexual addictions affect children, teens, adults, and even the elderly in a frightening and unprecedented way. Degenerative diseases unpredictably attack and inexorably devastate the most robust constitutions, while a burning desire for pleasure and power dominates many minds that want them at any cost.

Indeed, there are millions of well-meaning people concerned with the violent eruption of today's challenges that threaten love and ethics, as if intending to push everything and everyone into chaos all at once.

A massive wave of agony smashes and submerges society's coastline, decimating its most beautiful constructions.

Feeling like demigods, modern men and women dream of becoming the new Divinity, manipulating the DNA to completely alter the human constitution, eventually producing monsters, saints, mentally handicapped individuals or sages at will; cloning other individuals to satisfy the scientific and social *needs of the times, believing themselves capable of changing the course of psycho-anthropological evolution from that moment on. They contemplate resuscitating cadavers by employing techniques that could dribble past death, making the physical body almost perpetual —as if the body could resist time and its wear and tear. These are but a few of the many projects in which many researchers and ambitious dreamers are involved.*

Materialistic ideas still prevail in universities and research labs seeking to deny the Spirit and its causality, thereby reducing human beings to be the product of molecular whims, and human thought to neural determinisms that cerebral anoxia reduces to nothing.

Nevertheless, life surprises all of us with its inexhaustible potential, which the mind remains powerless to probe in its entirety. This fact invites us to engage in deep reflection regarding the limits within which we operate, and the imponderability of the events that amaze us on a daily basis.

After all, science per se has never actually created anything, since everything science puts forth is somehow an imperfect copy of what scientists observe in the grand canvas of Creation.

Slowly but surely, facts previously brushed aside by human presumptuousness began to gain so much attention that there was no other alternative than to observe and study them. The conclusion was that immortality is real; that the Spirit preexists and survives death; that there is a God-created cosmic order; and that a moral and ethical sense is of paramount importance to a happy life.

Equally honorable and sincere scholars and researchers have been lowering their probes into the very essence of the facts, thereby concluding that beings are thinking energy endowed with an individual psychology and physiology outside the material realm. Unbeknownst to them, by said conclusions scholars and researches ultimately became apostles of the Spirit.

They are the missionaries of the living faith from the past that now return within the scientific field to confirm that the destiny of beings is eternal glory.

For all these reasons, these are glorious days.

✳

In this book, we have gathered current topics that have stirred up controversy in different academic and religious circles, to present our observations and opinions found on the consoling teachings of Spiritism with its triple aspect as a science, a philosophy, and a religion. Spiritism was received from Humanity's Guides. Allan Kardec,[1] who further contributed with his profoundly wise and judicious observations as well as with his irrefutable logic, codified it.

We are aware that many students of Spiritism have seriously pondered about the topics covered in this book, and therefore have clear and objective answers. We treat such information with the seriousness and the respect it deserves.

Our goal is just somehow to contribute so that the incomparable teachings of Spiritism may be taken into consideration, for Spiritism restores and refreshes Jesus' thoughts —always alive and vibrant in the hearts and minds of all who love Him.

Salvador, October 19th, 1998
JOANNA DE ÂNGELIS

---

1. Allan Kardec (1804-1869). Pen name of Hippolyte Léon Denizard Rivail, Codifier of the Spiritist Doctrine. – Tr.

1

SCIENTIFIC ADVANCES

An upsurge of scientific advances –particularly the successive inventions of the past century– has unquestionably changed the way we live.

Ideas propounded by brave men and women such as Allan Kardec, Charles Darwin, Karl Marx, Sigmund Freud, Marie Curie, and Albert Einstein have so revolutionized our habits and ideas that we are still trying to adapt to the new world they have uncovered.

In regard to technology –from the steam locomotive to the telephone– the world underwent a tremendous change that entirely transformed the current structure up to that point.

The medical field expanded its frontiers with the discovery of anesthesia, asepsis, microbiology, and vaccines that have saved millions of lives that otherwise would have been lost to diseases without a cure.

Microsurgery techniques enhanced the healthcare arsenal even further by safely repairing delicate brain components and other essential organs.

The new and valuable information that humans have gained about the cosmos and human physiology, however, did not answer their questions. Instead, even more complex issues arose waiting for future observations and research.

In their naïveté, scientists of the past had quick answers to almost every question presented to them, which not always corresponded to the reality of the facts. As the human perception of the universe expanded and the research focused on the essence of atomic and subatomic particles, understanding and adequately utilizing their almost infinite possibilities became more difficult.

The very human mind remains a mystery to neurophysiologists who struggle to delineate the region of the brain where the mind manifests, as they struggle with memory and its mechanisms to retain complex and, often, abstract information by processes of biochemical interactions that can be activated by a simple act of the will.

The discovery of the axon, for example, has allowed us to understand the neurons in the brain. However, the latest findings concerning interleukins, cerebrins, interferons, and other enzymes have broadened almost infinitely our understanding of nerve mechanisms and their important functions for human beings, their thinking ability, memory, and homeostasis, among others.

Concomitantly, the identification of the location where mind-body interaction takes place –the limbic-hypothalamic area– given the high neuron presence, explained the reason why this area lies at the base of the brain and atop the spine, allowing for the perfect communication of the Spirit with the body and vice versa.

More advanced studies within this field gave us an understanding of how these psychophysical interactions are processed. Said studies have demonstrated that higher sentiments, such as love, solidarity, trust, benevolence, tenderness, charity, and faith could correspond to the presence of photons in the body. Conversely, negative or primitive feelings such as hatred, resentment, fear, anguish, rage, jealousy, and envy could appear as electrons. As a result, we have either well-being or ill-being depending on the type of mental wave in which individuals linger.

Concurrently, molecular biology —broadening its observations— has also leaped to unprecedented heights demonstrating that psychical factors are essential for physical balance and vice versa. It has shown that the human structure is a consequence of a person's mental and moral behavioral pattern.

Quantum Physics has already demystified matter, heading triumphantly toward energy and reaching the subtle fabric of the Spirit, which is the *intelligent principle of the Universe*. Furthermore, it is very close to identifying the causal world from which all things originate.

Having *discovered* the Spirit, transpersonal psychology and sister therapies have found answers and treatments to solve old and challenging problems that remain as such in other schools. They have also made mental and behavioral life more ennobling and enticing propositions with fascinating possibilities to bring about peace and a state of plenitude.

Life reigns sovereign everywhere, even in the mineral kingdom where it *sleeps* dreaming of unknown latent possibilities.

Despite these unrivaled scientific and technological breakthroughs, we remain challenged by a significant number of issues waiting for answers from the scientific world. Is there life beyond Earth? Why is it impossible for the brain to interpret itself? What is behind the biological determinism that causes cells to die or *commit suicide* in order to maintain the physical form without exceeding the limits imposed by equilibrium? On a more distant note: What are *black holes?* What happened before the Big Bang? Given the presence of *quasars,* created by the encounter between returning and forward-moving particles, does the universe have limits? What about dark energy, which despite permeating everything is yet to be photographed? Again, these are but a few of many other questions, for there is still a significant number of other phenomena in the macrocosms and the microcosms...

Slowly, and even unbeknownst to them, scientists become apostles of the Spirit, and courageously advance to find God and His omnipresent Laws.

Spiritism, in turn, as an *observational* science, has already penetrated these *mysteries* offering logical solutions that originate in the Divine Reality; the immortal Spirit and its reincarnations; animic[2] and mediumistic phenomena; ethical and moral principles; and the legacy of Jesus' teachings: love, forgiveness, charity, renunciation of human passions, true humility, compassion, and mercy, in order to offer humans peace and security as it propels them along the path of integration with the Cosmic Consciousness.

The day when science and religion will hold hands, mutually completing each other, is slowly approaching. Equally anchored on facts, reason, and logic –which must be their foundation– they will quickly conquer deeper values and interpretations concerning life and the infinite.

This will only be possible because of reincarnation, as it allows Spirits to return to the physical body to continue with

---

2. Animic: In Spiritism, it refers to psychic phenomena produced by the incarnate Spirit without the intervention of other Spirits (e.g. telepathy, telekinesis, psychometry, among others). – Tr.

their cherished studies and endeavors, for which death is not an interruption. On the contrary, Spirits return even better prepared –by the memories of the real world acquired during the errant state[3]– to apply such knowledge on the earth that helps to overcome pernicious atavisms and passions to which they became enslaved during their transit along the primitive evolutionary stages.

The universe is the condensation of God's Love, and while intelligence will allow us to understand it, only love will enable us to feel it.

The harmony created by the union of knowledge and sentiment is called wisdom, which is a high-level achievement that all humans will have to attain. Allan Kardec referred to it as *intellectual and moral plenitude.*

---

3. Errant State: The interval between incarnations in the spirit world. For more in-depth information see "Spirit Life," Ch. VI, Questions 223-23, *The Spirits' Book* by Allan Kardec (International Spiritist Council, 4th Edition, Revised (2010)). –Tr.

2
MENTAL FORCES

The mind is a dynamo of hard-to-catalog energy that radiates automatically according to its inherent emotional content. An exteriorization of the Spirit, it is interpreted by the brain that converts it into an idea. As such, it becomes a vehicle for communication of various kinds. It is a radiating force whose vibratory rate is determined by the sender's sentiments.

Even when unconsciously emitted, mental energy attunes to equivalent mental energy, producing effects that correspond to its intrinsic nature.

Somewhat known almost throughout history, it has been used in different ways, almost always reaching its goal.

After careful study, Mesmer discovered its therapeutic possibilities giving us Animal Magnetism (Mesmerism). Utilizing his valuable resources, the Marquis of Puységur succeeded in transmitting this force to the trees, which once magnetized, temporarily held and transferred the vibrations. Allan Kardec worked with magnetism and was able to help subjects reach somnambulic states while Dr. James Braid was able to reach hypnotic states. As our knowledge about this force evolved, we were able to probe it deeper and understand it better. As a result, we were in a position to find explanations for a whole host of phenomena previously seen as miraculous or supernatural.

It is the vehicle for many animic phenomena because it originates in the Spirit, which emits is like an antenna that never ceases to vibrate. Likewise, it answers for the different instances of telepathy, telekinesis –spontaneous movement of objects– and natural combustion. The power of the mind is a neglected, powerful agent available to human beings who have not known how to use it properly.

Due to the subtle nature of the waves it exteriorizes, the mind is involved in the constructions of the physical world and acts directly on all bodies, sometimes altering their constitution. The same applies to psychical exchanges, as mental waves act on similar bandwidths and produce effects that correspond with their vibrational rate.

The universe is a product of the Divine Mind, whose beneficial action never ceases.

Everything that surrounds human beings is, in a certain way, the product of their mental affinities. They are also co-creators, on account of the constructions they erect with the continuous emissions of their psychical power.

At the same time, this energy is responsible for countless instances of well-being and ill-being; health and sickness; enthusiasm and apathy.

Mental energy penetrates all obstacles; it covers distances at incredible speed and easily reaches the target, which almost always offers resonance.

Mental exchanges are much more prevalent than we can imagine. Whether consciously or unconsciously, they take place between men and women; between people and animals or plants; between Spirits, some of whom use them appropriately; between Spirits and human beings as well as with the Source of Life.

Indecent aspirations and desires; resentment and hatred; jealousy and passions are radiating sources of low-level mental energy that travel in the direction of people and anything else that might be the target.

Emotional and behavioral disturbances, sluggishness, irascibility, tension, and anguish often times derive from negative energy released by imbalanced minds as they intensely vibrate toward their disaffections.

Negativity, self-deprecation, and pernicious stimulations also answer for nervous imbalances, depression, and inner torments caused by the absorption of sickly mental waves.

Joy, idealism, and ennobling achievements are generated and sustained by a mind that is attuned to the universal order, which in turn, also vitalizes the sender.

The mind exerts incomparable power during the physical existence. How such power is used determines whether civilization flourishes or deteriorates.

The cultivation of anesthetizing or toxic thoughts inflicts unsuspected damages upon individuals themselves, their immediate circle, and the society in which they live. The same happens when thoughts are of an elevated nature, filled with hope and productive ideas. They generate ongoing positive change in individuals, their immediate circle, and society as a whole.

The more we stimulate the mind by focusing on a specific idea, the more preponderant this idea becomes, beginning to control every aspiration in connection with the human being and its life.

Great inventors and innovators throughout history are a great example. By forging strong bonds with idealistic goals and living by them they continued to grow and produce even more.

The opposite is also true, but in a more critical manner. The vices and unhealthy behaviors that dominate the mental landscape and gradually intensify consume their victims, who are always empty, unfulfilled, malnourished, and sickly.

The pattern of our lives is always a consequence of the pattern of our thoughts. This is because in addition to the effects that mental waves have on their agent, they attune with equivalent vibrations, thereby creating a greater, more powerful wave that causes enormous suffering and depletion.

Damaging mental exchanges predominate on the earth among the people. However, there are also stimulating, affectionate, and enhancing psychical influences that cross the distances, and are received by the intended recipients within the same wavelength.

Any kind of motion and construction taking place in the world is the product of mental forces traveling from one psychical antenna to another; from one place to another; building and demolishing; starting or stopping projects.

Envelop yourself in good thoughts and pray always, so that your psychical forces may be of the positive kind.

Prayer affords attunement with the high-frequency radiations of the Divine Mind, which will infuse and benefit you.

However, if you remain uninformed about psychical exchanges and you are not vigilant, you will suffer the harmful effect of many minds that seek you out to steal your vitality or impose upon you not always healthful influence, which will overpower you.

Whether you want to or not, you are always attuning with mental forces that move about in the world. Your emotional identity produces emissions that connect you with others of identical vibrational rate.

Do not neglect the nature of our thoughts and aspirations, the things you say, and how you act. All of that originates in the mind and, should your mind be undisciplined and unaccustomed to prudent behavior, you will suffer the effects of reciprocity.

You breathe in an atmosphere saturated by your psyche, living according to its radiations. If you ascend to higher planes, you will be nourished by pure and healthy energy. If you descend into the pit of lustful and lascivious desires, you will be intoxicated by its natural morbid emanations.

You choose the psychical realm in which you live and pursue self-realization.

Many times, you will come across psychical minefields littered with toxic and dangerous energy, magnetized by perverse and sickly spiritual beings that use other people to get to you and cause you harm.

During such battles, your moral resources, stemming from your psychical energy, are all you have. It will be thanks to such vigorous emissions that you will escape from them, for they fear nothing else.

Therefore, grow stronger through self-knowledge, increasing your ability to think correctly in order to act even more appropriately, gaining self-control and finding a sure path for your existence on the earth.

Your thoughts are a fountain of life that you cannot neglect.

Your mental forces must be cared for, amplified, and applied to implement new behaviors for yourself and the world, under the inspiration of Jesus Christ, whose earthly existence was always lived in perfect attunement with God, from whom He received the strength for His ministry, and to maintain His ascendancy over evil *entities* –loaded with destructive energy– whom He very often had to face.

3
MIND-BODY INTERACTION

The human being is a miniature universe, in which every individual component is equally important for the harmony of the whole. Any attempt to study it under only one aspect will yield incomplete results, due to the absence of factors that are essential for an accurate identification of its reality.

For this very reason, it is not possible to separate mind from body and vice versa, in other words, Spirit from matter.

The influence of the psyche on the physical body is paramount to living a well-balanced life.

A sound state of mind reflects on the physical body as well-being because the emissions of the psychical factory lubricate the cellular machinery which starts to run smoothly.

Every day, scientists within the medical field gather increasing evidence attesting to this fact –which had been already identified during the early days of the art of healing, mainly once the Greek fathers of medicine understood that the mind is of outmost importance to living in balance.

The latest findings in psychology have demonstrated that psychosocial factors play a very prominent role in human behavior. Heredity is of lesser importance than education, interpersonal relationships, economic pressures, and manifestations of affection, which program the individual for either happiness or unhappiness. Consequently, happiness or unhappiness has a strong impact on a person's health, by either enabling the onset of disease or preserving overall well-being.

Stressful behaviors; the habitual repression of aggressive emotions; the tension resulting from outer compliance and internal rebellion; an accumulation of resentment or afflicting passions; unchecked ambition and a lack of self-love become toxic substances produced by a brain suffering the effects of mental distress. Such poisons spread through the central nervous system, ultimately taking hold in different parts of the body —especially those that are more sensitive— such as the gastric, respiratory, and reproductive systems, where they wreak havoc.

Conversely, feelings of hope, faith, love, joy, peace and uplifting ideas produce abundant emissions of salutary energy, which carried by peptide molecules in the form of endorphins, interferon, interleukins, and other equivalent substances, restore balanced mitosis by reversing damage, stimulating leucocytes, and setting up circuits of well-structured vibrations.

Love, for example, is physiological, even though it manifests as a sentiment of the deep self, since —from a quantum perspective— it can be detected as photons, whereas fear and ire can be detected as electrons.

Thought plays an important role in the entire human existential machinery, as it passes through all the cells, mainly those of the sympathetic nervous system, which maintain a perfect interaction with the cells of the immune system.

Thus, mental emissions travel by way of the referred peptide molecules through both systems producing effects in conformity with the nature of their inherent waves.

Mind-body interaction results, in turn, from the fact that the human constitution is not just material, but essentially psychophysical, and thus t is the work of the Spirit in its capacity as the intelligent and organizing agent in the human being.

Through brain neurons and their electrochemical connections, the Spirit continuously sends all kinds of messages to every corner of the body through which it manifests.

When the said emissions are made up of optimistic, appeasing, and serenely joyful ideas, the body experiences a positive response that makes it dynamic and youthful. Its components are well preserved.

On the other hand, when these emissions are loaded with deleterious, depressive, restless, and perturbing energies, the body experiences a damaging effect, as this type of energy attacks the immune system and overthrows the balance responsible for health.

So, in this context, health is more than just the absence of disease, for disease will always appear in different ways as a consequence of the need to transcend that every individual must face during his or her evolutionary process.

No sooner do we come up with the resources to eradicate one disease, another no less severe or threatening one appears. Such has been the case on the earth for thousands of years because the Spirits inhabiting the planet are still somewhat backward in nature –with natural exceptions– and, therefore, require the scourge of suffering to achieve purification and develop the potential wealth of light lying dormant within them.

Since suffering is not the purpose of physical life but to provide humans with an opportunity to further develop their internal resources and to work with themselves to overcome painful predicaments, these two tasks cannot be postponed. The effort required to fulfill them allows humans to accurately manage every situation that affects them negatively, generating distress and unhappiness.

In light of the Spirit's command over the cellular organization, mind-body interaction must help individuals achieve self-healing, just as it leads to self-realization all those who use the means to obtain release from emotional strain and unwarranted fear.

We will certainly not find self-healing mechanisms for every disease, for this would require a certain psychical and emotional behavioral structure, which has not yet been achieved by most human beings. However, this is not important. The critical part is how individuals behave and use the available resources to grow and attain self-realization – which can be done regardless of whether they have a disease or not. In fact, people in reasonably good health often fail.

Standing to inherit its own legacy along the string of successive incarnations, the Spirit carries within the successes and the failures sustained in past illuminative experiences. Some of these effects catch up to the Spirit as an invitation to repeat the experience, to reflect, to move past the limitation from which it needs to break free. This is why Spirits are frequently burdened by emotional, psychical and physical conditions that become very heavy crosses to bear. However, as a Spirit changes the nature of its mental life and adheres to a moral code of conduct the road conditions gradually improve, and it begins to experience well-being. At this point, the Spirit is prepared to manage the remaining typical aggravations of the physical journey.

No one living in the world is without challenges, particularly relating to health, interpersonal relationships, personal aspirations, and the processes of inner growth. It is these very challenges that promote all beings; develop their capacity to fight and to improve, helping them to always achieve higher evolutionary levels, without which life on earth would ultimately lose its purpose and spiritual meaning.

Consequently, making life as agreeable as possible and turning it into an enriching experience —full of personal triumphs— is the intelligent attitude of all who become aware of the transient nature of the body and the permanent nature of the Spirit.

Through self-illumination and a predisposition to use the power of the mind over the body, human beings start living a well-delineated physical existence, learning to face every event naturally and with an ethical disposition to win.

Indeed, we do not imply passively accepting the adverse events that take place during the course of an incarnation. In that case, our apparent resignation would be nothing more than an escape valve to conceal feelings of disappointment and revolt, which take hold as internal conflicts that will reflect on the somatic organism in the future.

The idea is to *digest* and accept everything that happens, allowing our inner peace to prevail over perturbing and violent events, which seem to discourage individuals from staying engaged in the struggle.

Par excellence, human beings are what they think about and cultivate in their mental field, which ultimately materializes. Structurally made up of vital fluid, and as the *intelligent principle of the Universe,* their essence is highly psychical and is in constant interaction with their physical organization.

Therefore, a healthy individual is not someone who is ecstatic —someone who looks as though he or she has won every confrontation to date— but someone who continues to fight, always willing to keep an eye on the future ahead.

The importance of mind-body interaction will become so evident to the medical field that, in the future, genetic engineering will work on substances that support health and generate self-healing. These lab-synthesized substances will be made into products readily available to the public. However, holding on to peace or reaping the sick pleasure of living in constant turmoil will always be a matter of personal choice.

4
MENTAL ENERGY AND A HEALTHY LIFE

It is up to the intelligent being on the earth to discover the fundamental reason for its own existence, in order to set parameters conducive to happiness and develop the capacity for inner growth –the main purpose of self-realization. Until it decides to identify and implement the most compatible methods for moral and spiritual enrichment, everything will seem devoid of meaning or transformative power, making the physical journey into a challenge filled with disappointment and affliction.

Still harboring in the deep unconscious all the conflicts characteristic to the process of rational development to which it was subjected –dark and painful episodes, repression enforced by ignorance, and the fear inherent to life's primitive stages– individuals are more likely to yield to morbid states of depression, anxiety, and insecurity than to be enraptured by the enchantment of ennobling aspirations, beauty, and peace, which must encourage them to achieve victory in the most varied existential situations.

Joy should be the spontaneous behavioral norm in all thinking beings, even when circumstances are not in line with their wishes, since day-to-day occurrences change from one minute to the next, turning sadness into delight and happiness into misfortune.

The very fact that someone enjoys the blessing of being in a physical body is a gift –even if it is a body marked by problems and limitations– because it provides an opportunity to self-transcend altering the personal landscape –something that depends exclusively on choosing good behavior.

In this instance, as well as in others, the mind plays a relevant role in behavior because it writes every program to which the body submits. Its effective action propagates through waves that reach the delicate mechanisms of the neuropeptides, which branch out into the central nervous system, the immune system, and the endocrine system –all of them interdependent– communicating with all the cells in the somatic organization.

However, deeply scarred by past life unresolved problems, individuals almost always become the spontaneous victims of reemerging fixations that imprint purifying conflicts in the area of emotions, to which individuals cling to out of a psychological need for self-punishment –something entirely unnecessary for a truly healthy and happy life from an evolutionary point of view.

A stubborn attitude that keeps the emotions in a state of confusion answers for the untold suffering to which a person submits, as he or she begins to live masochistically without being aware of the disturbance behind it.

A desire for what is right, beautiful, peaceful, and joyful signals a conscience that has awakened and is ready to reach new heights.

Controlled by the mind, the brain responds according to the type of orders it receives, either contributing with enzymes that support health or with toxins that destroy the sensitive equipment of the physical, emotional, or mental machinery.

The mind, however, can be the victim of habits that become ingrained and turn into degenerative factors for the thinking being. It is thus indispensable that it be renewed, cultivating elevated ideas that foster well-being.

Understandably, the body will be affected, from time to time, by viruses and bacilli or by problems of some kind or another, even if the person is perfectly attuned to wholesome ideas. This is a natural occurrence.

The very material constitution that clothes the real being is fragile and, therefore, susceptible of suffering various natural disturbances and degenerative processes due to its propensity to undergo constant transformations –including the dissolution of the cellular archipelago through which it manifests. Otherwise, we would have the immortality of the form, which is always changing and is headed for decomposition. What matters, however, is the state of mind of an individual when dealing with its physical apparatus, maintaining an atmosphere of optimism and harmony.

A disease often plays a significant role in human behavior. First, it renders evident the body's fragility. Second, it invites humans to reflect about its causes. Lastly, it provides an opportunity to learn how to manage all existential phenomena.

So, we ask ourselves how to deal with suffering when it arises. We can reject it pure and simple, detest it out of rebelliousness, or accept it with resignation boarding on indifference. It is possible, however, to use a different kind of approach –one that is dynamic.

Rejection is in no way able to change the situation. If anything, it makes it harder for the person to receive the message that suffering brings and contributes to render the problem bigger and more complex. A rebellious response depletes the reserves of equilibrium and strength, intensifying the affliction. A passive and indifferent resignation that does not work for the eradication of the problem's causes is pathological and must be fought against; it is discouragement that takes hold of the person. Only an attitude of acceptance in which individuals understand the painful event and strive to change the outcome –moving past limitations and remaining committed to their goals despite the magnitude of the effort– contributes in the structuring of intelligent beings, as they learn the lessons that always follow any kind of trial or painful event.

For this reason, the help that hope provides is essential because it fosters courage, which derives from a higher, positive, and empowering mental vibration that emanates from life itself.

The Spirit experiences a physical journey to develop its entire potential still in germ-like form. Thus, the Spirit remains connected to the Higher Source from where it comes, which inspires and motivates it as it faces all the vicissitudes it will inevitably encounter. The Spirit will always grow through harmonious processes, that is, equilibrium and behavioral changes –which certainly does not mean maladjustment– but that will develop new skills to face the circumstances and challenges inherent to the evolutionary process.

This entire program is possible if individuals embrace self-knowledge, discovering their reality, which exceeds the limits of the physical body and extends along the path of immortality. As the next step, they establish existential goals, the purpose and objectives of the human journey, striving to achieve the goal —even if in small increments— without stressful haste or mortifying delays.

A lucid mind propels beings toward endless progress, radiates messages that strengthen them, and helps them maintain the balance that characterizes real health —the kind of health that lasts even as they go through periods of sickness, afflictions or disturbances of any kind. Rooted deep within the individual, this state of well-being is what predisposes individuals to invest in joyful new attempts to conquer happiness.

The goal is to keep the mind in harmony with the cosmos to set up a suitable plan for the human being to evolve.

So, in whatever situation the thinking being might be, its source of physical emissions must be in perfect attunement with the waves of the Divine Psyche, from which they receive all of life's endowments as well as the means to attain every existential objective.

5

THOUGHTS AND ILLNESSES

The human conscience reaches every corner of the body through the different rates of vibration inherent to the body's components.

Thus –working in overall harmony– each cell possesses an individual budding conscience in whose delicate mesh are imprinted the evolutionary needs of the human being.

Influenced by the automatic commands sent by the perispirit[4], cells result from the condensation of specific waves that carry a Spirit's moral content, which are in turn tasked

---

4. Perispirit: Allan Kardec's terminology for what is also known as the astral body. See questions 93-95, *The Spirits' Book* by Allan Kardec (International Spiritist Council, 4th Edition, Revised (2010)). [Excerpts from Questions 93-95: "Is the spirit per se without a covering, or as some insist, is it surrounded by some kind of substance?" "*The spirit is surrounded by a substance that might look vaporous to you, but which is still quite dense to us. Nevertheless, it is sufficiently vaporous to be able to raise itself up into the air and travel to wherever it wants to go.*" As a fruit seed is surrounded by the perisperm, the spirit per se is surrounded by an envelope, which, by comparison, may be called the perispirit . . . . [This semi-material envelope has a specific form] *and that is how it sometimes appears to you in dreams or in a waking state and how it may take on a visible or even tangible form.*"] – Tr.

with creating the organs and the different mechanisms of an individual's organism.

The cell therefore is, per se, the materialization of the energy blueprint elaborated by the *biological organizing model*[5].

The molecular disaggregation of each cell at the time of death is not the disintegration or annihilation of the underlying energy, which continues to be an integral part of the organizing whole. Consequently, each cell has specific registers that synchronize into a harmonic whole. This type of register can be considered a form of embryonic *conscience* that transmits and saves *information* in connection with experiences in which it participates.

Accordingly, the perispirit is also made up by the agglomeration of said *cellular consciences,* which in turn compose the global conscience, whose job it is to transmit to the Spirit its memories, achievements, and realizations experienced during each incarnation –as well as all of them combined– always altered by the natural transformations occurring at every stage.

As the thoughts derived from the spiritual being transfer to the areas of sensation, emotion, and action, they imprint their content in the *energy cells*[6] mentioned above, which enact them in the world of form, producing results in keeping with the quality of the mental wave.

Thanks to the rate of vibration of each mental emission, the charge stimulates the cellular *conscience* that is either strengthened –thereby supporting health– or is disharmonized –thereby promoting disease. Even when the structure of the

---

5. BOM: Biological Organizing Model. Another term for the perispiritual body or perispirit. – Tr.
6. Energy cells: "Células de energia" in the Portuguese original. The author refers to the energy counterpart of the physical cell. – Tr.

physical cell comes undone, the energy cell is released during the process of cellular disaggregation, which will influence the future mechanisms of balance or imbalance in the human being.

The most severe diseases are those that originate in the soul, spreading through the physical organism and becoming degenerative and infectious processes, which either cause physical pain or exteriorize as conflicts that develop into psychical disorders, whose gravity depends on the causing factor.

The cultivation of hatred, jealousy, envy, ire, and other assorted anesthetics of the Spirit produces psychical viruses and vibrios that attack the body of the host and that of the person who —unguarded— inspired the production of such devastating waves —which the mind produces according to its moral constitution. Concomitantly, ideoplasties[7] sustained by thoughts fixated on disturbing and violent ideas contribute to the emergence of toxins that invade the body, upsetting its vibrational structure, causing it to become ill, and working to destroy its defenses, its immunological factors.

Mental behavior expresses the evolutionary stage in which each being lingers and is responsible for generating well-being or ill-being; health or sickness; joy or sadness —always the result of the wavelength in which the person remains.

The bizarre behaviors in which many people indulge, transfer from one existence to another thanks to the *memory* and the *conscience* of the psychical cell, that, in turn, molds its physical counterpart in the future, according to its intrinsic energy. So, this wave will influence individuals since their genetic formation, altering their structure according to the type of message it brings.

---

7. Ideoplasties: In Spiritism, the thought forms created by the action of the mind upon matter. – Tr.

Diseases of the soul are psychical in nature and can be found in the recesses of the unsound mind, which is tied to aberrant behavioral states when it could be focused toward achieving balance, reason, and happiness.

Vile sentiments open the door to the onset of such diseases, for which diagnosis is difficult, treatment is deficient, and patient recovery is unlikely.

Thus, irresponsible sexual behavior, vices of all kinds, irritability, and negativity become *living agents* that act in accordance to the aim received from the mental dynamo where they originate.

The same would happen if different sentiments and ethical principles that promote human beings were cultivated, for they would see to reciprocate their source with waves of well-being, hope, harmony, happiness, etc.

The chromosomes that are implanted in the physical structure through the cell nucleus where they get established remain connected to the Spirit, thanks to the cytoplasm to which they attach. Indestructible, they send their messages via the genetic nucleus as they mold the future living forms of all beings, whether in the physical or the spiritual realm.

The more scientific research lowers its probe into the structure of form, the more it verifies that it is an agglutination of particles that become progressively smaller to the point of getting *lost* in energy, which is the starting point of matter.

Since the Spirit is *thinking energy,* the *intelligent principle of the universe,* it assimilates the subtlest vibrations and externalizes them through mental waves that materialize, thus becoming an integral part of the whole through which physical life expresses itself.

Consequently, when a patient dies, the vices that gave rise to the diseases of the soul —which linger as depression, inner torments, anguish, insecurity, etc.— remain affixed to the person's psychical fields where they originated, requiring a corresponding amount of time to change the person's mindset in order to dissolve and disappear.

The biological phenomenon of death does not grant freedom from long-standing sick and perverse habits that were intensely nurtured during a long physical existence. Just as these habits took hold slowly and forged conditionings that progressed into perturbing conditions, the rebalancing and reconstruction process of the affected energy structures demand a comparable amount of time for the damaged vibratory fields to recompose.

This is understandable because the discharges triggered by vile sentiments produce toxins with high concentrations of hormones that alter the DNA codes, to which they affix their corresponding type of wave and morbid provenance. As this process is repeated over and over, the damage to the internal structure of the DNA gets worse, imposing – from beyond the grave– a total change in behavior that is responsible for the construction of the *double helix,* which are two intertwined *strands* made up by a specific chemical substance.

So, diseases of the soul will only be cured when there is a structural modification of peoples' thoughts, which in turn will build new super-subtle foundations that will consubstantiate in future DNA codes, restoring the *individual consciences* of the cells and, ultimately, integrating the conscience of the human being into the Cosmic Conscience's harmonic whole.

6

DISEASES OF THE SOUL

A s an ensemble of very delicate components necessary to perform its tasks, the human brain remains largely unknown at its essence, despite a number of remarkable scientific breakthroughs.

From Galen's old theory of *The Four Humors* to Gall's demonstrations through Phrenology –including the deep understanding of neurons and their functions as well as the admirable findings about the roles of the left and the right hemispheres– a massive body of knowledge has already been gained.

Still, an infinite number of functions are yet to be mapped out, just as their relationships with the mental, behavioral, emotional and, physical life of human beings is yet to be established.

As far as health is concerned, the brain's action is decisive because it is the decoder of human thought and directs this extraordinary wave of barely-known energy, but which is nonetheless responsible for setting the course of a physical existence.

The Spirit activates and controls the brain, slowly taking over all of the brain's inherent resources. Consequently, the complex mechanisms that predispose individuals to a state of balance or to the various dysfunctions that perturb them – manifesting as the most varied types of illnesses– find in the Spirit their point of origin.

This is so because through the perispirit –which transmits the evolutionary *needs* thanks to the impressions retained in its tenuous vibratory fabric– the Spirit emits equivalent mental waves that transform into healthy or unhealthy thoughts.

As the command center of the entire somatic organization, the brain processes degenerative phenomena as well as resistance mechanisms to fight against bacteriological life through the immune system, assimilating or eliminating karmic factors deriving from past life actions.

Consequently, it opens the door to the torments experience by a guilty conscience that become engraved as a self-obsession, reliving damaging or terrifying past life events from which the Spirit could not obtain release. At other times, the Spirit becomes easy prey to tormenting, acoustic, thought-waves sent by powerful adversaries from both planes of life or from distraught affections that have transformed a passion for sensuality into unhealthy appeals that negatively affect their target –when the target lacks inner harmony, does not cultivate the healthy habit of prayer and of thinking edifying thoughts, all of which render the individual impermeable to these continuous emissions.

Concomitantly, depressive states that generate pessimistic and nefarious thoughts largely contribute to the worsening of the neurotic disorder, just as they create the conditions for the establishment of harmful spirit obsessions[8],

---

8. Spirit obsession: The domination that certain Spirits acquire over certain individuals. *The Mediums' Book*, by Allan Kardec, Ch. XXIII, #237 (International Spiritist Council (2007)). – Tr.

when not of phenomena that deteriorate the cellular machine, facilitating the emergence of various illnesses.

Viruses incubate in the body for long periods of time but remain inactive until the host begins to emit waves that vitalize them, favoring their devastating and almost unstoppable proliferation.

In the case of HIV, for example, the virus in Acquired Immune Deficiency Syndrome (AIDS) –which entered the human body due to sexual promiscuity and is now a grave threat to society because a person can become infected through contaminated blood transfusions, the sexual act, and infected or shared needles during drug use– the mind of the victim plays a preponderant role in relation to its progression or its destruction. In this context, feelings of guilt, anger, lack of love, and rebelliousness have a preponderant negative influence, for they strengthen the disruptive virus as it attacks the body's defenses and facilitates the emergence of parasitic illnesses that, ultimately, destroy the physical life of their defenseless victims.

The same occurs with various types of malignant neoplasms, due to the existence of an *embryonic conscience* in the cell that is activated by the being's spiritual conscience. When a person gets cancer, if his or her mental life takes a turn for the worse –due to the presence of perturbing and toxic thoughts– it is plain to see why the resistance of the cellular *psychism* is defeated, allowing for the spread of the disease and, consequently, irreversible metastasis.

This is the case with all degenerative processes in the body –whether they may be caused by contamination, trauma, or genetic disorders. It is in a person's thoughts that we find the factors that can bring about at least a partial recovery when the disease is the effect of painful past life actions, or even a full recovery.

Jesus always advised those He healed to be careful, to refrain from sin and from contravening the harmony of the Law, so that nothing worse may befall them. He said so because bad behavior induces human thought to create the bad habit of cultivating perturbing ideas that begin to gravitate around their source, contributing to physical, psychical, and emotional imbalance.

Diseases of all kinds are anomalous states of the Spirit, which externalize in the body as a necessary purifying experience, so that the Spirit may restore its balance before the Greater Life –where it originates and of which it is a part.

Perhaps failing to recognize the fact that beings preexist the cradle and survive the grave, the World Health Organization (WHO) defines health as a state of physical, mental, and social well-being.

The absence of a disease does not imply health, however. Already present in an indebted Spirit, a disease travels slowly toward the body in which it will reveal itself. By the time it is identified by the pain it causes and the other disturbances it creates, the individual was already sick without knowing it. For as long as physical, mental and social well-being may be preserved, individuals can consider themselves to be healthy –and even if a few issues should arise, they can successfully go on by directing their mental resources appropriately, not allowing themselves to give in to despair or to morbid states that represent the diseases of the soul.

Health, therefore, is life's natural state.

Jesus never got sick that we know of, always appearing idealistic and balanced, even when pressured by absurd provocations or forced into useless debates much to the liking of sickly personalities of yesterday and today.

He never exempted Himself from work or from helping all those who looked for Him, demonstrating His perfect emotional stability and physical harmony as an Elevated Spirit whose entire trajectory was marked by love and ennobling actions.

It is, thus, in the recesses of the spiritual being that the *matrices* for the different diseases are to be found. So, it is there that diseases must be treated. Otherwise, though the consequences may be stopped momentarily, we would be but delaying the continuation of those pernicious and destructive events.

We can never emphasize enough that thoughts are the catalysts for every event concerning human beings. If by chance, said actions do not find their unleashing mental agent in the present, then it is to be found in the spiritual traveler's obscure *yesterday*.

Accordingly, it is imperative that thoughts be constantly renewed for the better, forging healthy habits and intensifying actions that generate blessings, so that a state of well-being may stand as a permanent divider between the different stages of human activity.

Naturally, everyone experiences multiple instances in which health breaks down, but this is no cause for concern. It has to do with the development of vital functions of the organism and the self-repairing mechanisms of internal parts, none of which causes any harm to the general harmony of mind and body.

7
RECOVERY AND CURE

It is critical to make a technical difference between a physical recovery and a cure. A physical recovery has to do with restoring the malfunctioning cellular equipment to proper function. However, it does not always mean that the patient's health has returned. A cure takes place at the level of the most delicate mechanisms within the cellular constitution.

The mechanisms responsible for physical deterioration and the onset of disease are located at the core of the being within its energy structure –for which the perispirit is responsible in its capacity as the organizing model of the form, and, therefore, of the critical needs for the evolution of the spiritual being.

Thanks to that subtle body composed of specific energy, the mental waves that derive from ideas systematically nurtured by an individual –which later consolidate as actions– imprint the factors that become responsible for the critical events that occur deep within the molecular structure of the physical body.

So with the beginning of the complex mechanism of shaping the biological organization –the cells, their structure, development, and their multiplication through mitosis as a natural result of an individual's intricate mental and moral processes– we have either a healthy or an ill individual, according to the person's evolutionary needs. This is how the programs in connection with each physical existence are set.

Consequently, human beings are the product of everything they create, cultivate, and do.

A real cure requires a profound inner transformation, which can only occur when the factors responsible for the painful predicament change for the better, thus restoring the balance at the energy level.

In that case, it is imperative that the mind processes all of its emotional and moral content adequately, so that the physical recovery brought on by the therapy applied may produce a real cure, avoiding relapses that derive precisely by the absence of vibrational balance among the delicate elements through which the Spirit interacts with the body.

A temporary recovery may be the result of the therapist's efforts, the right medication, and a momentary change in the patient's attitude. However, without a profound behavioral change –a sincere desire to be cured, the inner pursuit of well-being, lofty goals, and the renewal of mental habits– the disease will certainly return or will reemerge as a new disease fulfilling its task to awaken individuals to the fact that they are immortal beings.

In the vast majority of people who are ill, we see the consequence of a certain past life behavior at which time the person gave up on life's principles –even if unconsciously– as the result of events that could have been handled in a less pessimistic and self-destructive way.

A succession of misfortunes, frustrations, and existential disappointments is inevitable because such instances abound in the human experience. It is the person's response to these events that defines his or her future, even when there is subsequent emotional shift. Often, the damage to the delicate mesh of the equipment that generates the cells has already been done at the level of the energy that elaborates the molecules.

We notice that before the onset of the different diseases, the patient consented to the cultivation of inner turmoil, wished to abandon the material struggle, and felt exhausted by the succession of torments and moral suffering, giving in to the debilitating effects of discouragement.

The awareness about the spiritual reality helps us put forth the effort to continue to live in the body experiencing everything that has been reserved for us, knowing, however, that we will leave the body behind —as is natural— but only after having utilized all of the valuable resources provided by the very physical existence to lend it more dignity and make it more desirable.

This type of behavior significantly contributes to a quick recovery and a subsequent cure, even as the patient is eventually released from the physical machinery at the appropriate time.

In turn, the doctor must strive to uncover in the patient the real being suffering the effects of being in an unhealthy predicament, to start treating the person instead of merely treating the deficiency and offering the corresponding therapy. Such a medical contribution will also greatly help patients gain self-confidence and feel like human beings, rather than just bodies lying in a hospital bed or wherever they may be.

The complexity of human beings is firmly rooted in their emotions, in how they feel they are cared for, loved, and respected or —conversely— forgotten, disregarded, seen as a burden.

When people experience love, they feel encouraged and strive to correspond, provided that they have the psychological maturity that allows for lucid discernment. When this is not the case, they punish themselves, self-poisoning in one way or another, without even realizing it, or remain dominated by a desire to give up on their physical life.

Regardless of the kind of ailment devastating someone's body, words of encouragement, positive vibrations, and a jovial atmosphere become excellent –even indispensable– therapeutic contributions to help the patient achieve a physical recovery and regain their health, that is, attain a cure.

In this context, we might wonder why people who are notorious for their exceptional virtues, irreproachable conduct, and unquestionable adherence to highly ethical principles contract diseases, something that would apparently discredit the self-healing proposition as the result of leading a moral life and thinking high-minded thoughts.

The fact that individuals are a part of humankind, that is, they are covered in matter already indicates their transiency, thus emphasizing the opportunity to accomplish the self-illuminating experience.

What differentiates the average patient from another that has significant moral and emotional assets is how they accept and deal with problems, diseases, and existential challenges.

While the uninformed see suffering as a torment and a tragedy, others who are supported by a rational religious faith and emotional balance, see it as a tool for growth and an opportunity to acquire even more significant moral assets, something that is available only to those who are firmly committed to conquering the highest peaks of personal liberation.

Humankind counts its martyrs, heroes, saints, scientists, artists, philosophers, champions of the common good, and promoters of beauty among the people who –during different times throughout history– overcame their limitations.

They became examples of moral courage, spiritual greatness, and paradigms that serve as models for all those still stuck at the lower end of the evolutionary spectrum of human aspirations.

Above all of them, there is Jesus, who never got sick. Debt-free, He still sacrificed Himself to teach the rest of us sublimation and love at the highest-level human thought can conceive.

8
NEURONS AND CONSCIOUSNESS

The materialistic take on human beings –with its fatalistic approach on biological determinism– essentially provides a great stimulus to senselessness, perversity, and moral destabilization because it frees individuals from any responsibility in connection with their day-to-day lives.

Propounding that humans are guided by automatic biochemical processes in the brain leads to reductionism, by which individuals become what has already been designed in the innermost recesses of their neuronal configuration.

Consequently, benevolence, beauty, excellence, or criminality, immorality, indecorous behavior, and a tendency to achieve or to fail would all result from an inescapable deterministic imposition.

Psychosocial, socio-educational, and socio-economic factors might contribute to mitigating the circumstances and critical events with their consequences; however, they cannot change the existential course given this initial and disastrous fatalistic determination.

In addition to being chaotic, this concept is also convenient because it exempts people from personal effort and self-respect when they act aggressively, engage in criminal behavior or are vulgar.

An exclusively neuronal being will always be the victim of the dispositions of the equipment in the brain that make it an angel or a rebel, a genius or a monster.

The contributions of brain biochemistry in human existence, certainly cannot be disregarded. However, it is not the only cause behind success or failure, and morality or immorality because neurons were configured based on the messages that originate in the very subtle perispiritual meshes, in whose structural nets they find their genesis –the Spirit's accomplishments and defeats.

The fact that the conscience is a conquest of the Spirit and not a neuronal secretion changes the being's perspective in connection with responsibility to self, to life, and to Humanity, for it confers discernment, lucidity, and the freedom to choose.

Harmony or emotional, psychical, and physical instability originate in the immortal being, whose deeds are imprinted in its biological constitution through reincarnation.

Education is tasked with developing the latent values together with the support of the sentiments, creating the reality of each individual.

Biological determinism, therefore, is developed in the shape of the perispiritual energy, which allows cellular mitosis to reproduce in a way to adjust the organs to their inherent vibratory field.

Given that the mind is a faculty of the Spirit and not the brain – whose task it is to decode and calibrate it according to its possibilities for intellectual development– it is the mind that drives the process of reincarnation according to its own doing in past lives.

The mind thinks without the brain and communicates after the death of the body, whereas a damaged brain or a brain that does not receive the activity that originates in the mind is incapable of thinking.

Biochemical processes lack discernment to generate and select ideas, albeit said impulses can archive them in the recesses of memory, which are connected to the Spirit –where they originate– through very specific mechanisms.

Likewise, the changing levels of consciousness never result from the frequency of neuronal *hormones*, cerebrins, or other biological factors. It is the process of evolution that establishes each period as it stimulates individuals to conquer ever more significant and lofty goals.

The machine –whatever it may be– lacks spontaneity and does not function without the help of its builder. However complex and remarkable it may be, the machine cannot do without the human, while humans do not depend on the machine.

Brain impulses and neuronal synapses responsible for the preservation of physical life derive from the thinking agent that organizes and directs them, even when unaware of the process structured on the Laws of Life, which have established the mechanics of reincarnation.

Without a causal being, the temporal, organic assembly does not function.

For this reason, consciousness grows and develops as the Spirit acquires experience through its reincarnations. It would be impossible to make, in a single existence, the effort to reach the higher stages of evolution, the perfect integration with the Cosmic Consciousness. However, as we gradually gather experience and incorporate it into our intellectual and moral patrimony, there comes a time when our knowledge discerns and acts in consonance with the Divine Codes, at which point we start living in freedom.

All these achievements are impressed in the neurons in the brain through electrochemical processes made possible by the perispirit and which manifest in human behavior.

9

GENETIC ENGINEERING

T
he scientific advances taking place across the most diverse areas of knowledge demonstrate that human beings are progressing and reducing their burden of suffering –which they themselves program as the result of their negligence or ineptitude to deal with the necessary existential challenges.

The quest to overcome pain and all its consequences has been an ongoing effort, from the daring dreams to find the *philosopher's stone* in the Middle Ages, to ambitions that could turn into nightmares, such as penetrating the DNA to clone beings and other present-day unethical fantasies.

The Divinity, however, due the progress humans have made –particularly in the moral arena, and despite all the work still to be done in that respect– has allowed for the gradual mitigation of their most pungent afflictions, making room for better health, well-being, and joy, at the physical and psychical level.

Ever since the discovery of ether, chloroform, analgesics, and other pharmaceuticals, a great deal of brutal pain was dramatically diminished. Surgeries and microsurgeries have equally allowed people to continue living in the body without the severe limitations and deformities that were once the norm.

Indeed, much remains to be done in this area, which is why technological breakthroughs are made daily, offering more advanced and blessed therapeutic tools.

In Genetics, for example, ever since the discovery of genes and chromosomes by G. Mendel –who was reproached and brushed off by his contemporaries– breakthroughs are carefully catalogued to understand better the mechanisms of life at its origin, thus providing greater possibilities to help beings at the beginning stages and later on, as a result of their behavior.

Thanks to the almost infinite possibilities to penetrate the molecular organizations with the use of electronic microscopes, and the meticulous study of genes, scientists endeavor to accurately define the events of the physical and mental life, discovering how biological phenomena occur, human appearance and its details –from its configuration to eye and hair color– examining the intimate structures of the DNA and establishing norms to correct a number of anomalies.

Ignoring Life's superior mechanisms leads some of these noble researchers to dream fantastic dreams –at least for the time being– such as averting future degenerative diseases like cancer and AIDS by working on the genetic codes that present anomalies and create a propensity for the emergence of these diseases.

Alongside this decidedly respectable quest – but which cannot be part of the reincarnational program of many indebted Spirits, for if liberated from their afflictive constraint would incur other cleansing mechanisms – there is a number of Genetic Engineering enthusiasts thinking about the possibility of manipulating the complexity of these *organic microcomputers* to change the sex of the zygote, for example, or later that of the fetus, even as the shaping of the physical form is already underway.

The body, in whatever condition it may be, is the product of a Spirit's past behavior, which programs its needs in the human form to grow and evolve, transforming conflict into peace, debits into credits, and moral blemishes into hope.

Without questioning the human influence on the project, let us remember that the abuse of knowledge in any area always generates equivalent damages.

Let us look at what has been happening to the ecosystem, for instance. A lack of respect for nature, first out of ignorance and now out of despicable and financial interests, has caused a variety of dangerous effects for the very human existence. The destruction of the ozone layer has frightfully increased the number of skin cancer cases; the heavy use of chemical fertilizers in the soil has had very harmful effects on human health; the use of hormones in poultry and other animals is causing new diseases in human; the decrease of the water volume threatens regions where the existing life begins to die; the presence of mercury in rivers is poisoning them, destroying the flora, fauna, and riverbank populations; growing desertification and the melting of the polar caps are threats that worry a number of governments and nations of the planet that fear for the future –momentarily steeped in anguish.

Life is crafted by a principle of Divine Ethics that cannot be manipulated to cater to nonsense without unforeseeable consequences for the perpetrators.

Fascinated with the theoretical possibilities offered by Genetic Engineering, many researchers believe they can fool the Universal Laws, becoming small gods with unfathomable potential —which, incidentally, is understandable in the context of their materialistic fantasies through which they think everything can be reduced to the nothingness of the principle to which they turn to for support.

These researchers of the tangled secrets of planetary existence seem to think that they can *play God*, altering the genetic codes and creating aberrations to indulge their imagination. Clearly, human beings cannot even play human yet, since, every time they try, their game almost always results in devastating armed conflicts.

Understanding the immense possibilities within their reach, in 1990 several countries gathered a large number of international scientists in a daring project to decode the almost three billion characters found in the human cells as a result of their genetic code.

It is a noble task that has as its essential goal the understanding the molecular structure of the human being, and even finding a cure for afflictive diseases that devour lives. It was called *The Human Genome Project*, which, among other discoveries, confirmed that humans originated in Africa, from where they migrated all over the earth. Among several marvelous findings, it is now possible to demonstrate that there are no superior and inferior races, given that variations within the different ethnic groups are infinitely greater than previously thought, to the point where members of the same race present very different genetic characteristics. Likewise, it confirmed that black skin originated in regions where sunlight is very intense and, therefore, responsible for the dark pigmentation, which serves as defense and protection. Pigmentation becomes lighter as heat diminishes and, ultimately, turns white to synthesize vitamin D –necessary for the development of muscles and bones.

Following along this same line of observations, it is inevitable to corroborate that all that providential mechanism for organized human life has its template in the energy fields of the perispirit –that delicate envelope of the Spirit, which is life's real agent.

Concurrently, an urgent need arises for the presence of ethics in the form of limitations that must be imposed on the research, so that arbitrary governments and deranged individuals do not apply genetics' knowledge in macabre experiments such as the ones that took place, in the not-too-distant past, in concentration camps, where millions of lives perished without any dignity or compassion –or even humane feelings– at the hands of mad scientists who wanted to create a superior race in the vain presumption of subduing others they deemed inferior.

The inexorable march of time, or the being's voyage through the ever-flowing river of the present hours, has shown that only accomplishments in connection with the good, the beautiful, the honorable, or that generate dignity remain, while the utopia of madness dispels, like a dense fog in the heat of day.

Naturally, genetic engineering will be a tool to confer dignity to human beings and understand life in its most profound expressions, never a resource to subject humans to the passions and abuses of others that plan to put this knowledge to such nefarious ends.

10
HUMAN CLONING

Throughout time, the natural laws have improved the human form as a consequence of the moral progress attained. Slowly but precisely, biological and morphological traits appear more harmonious, obeying a plan conceived by the Spirit mentors of the earth, tasked with crafting the physical and psychical structures of life in their most varied expressions.

Since the perispirit and the physical body originate in the thinking energy, it is understandable that the more the essence improves, the subtler the covering becomes. Likewise, biological functions, which were initially programmed for the still violent circumstances of the earthly *habitat* and for the nutritional conditions that provided the fuel to live on the planet, also become more delicate and overcome past rigors.

Due to the natural transformations that have taken place in the earth's structure; due to the fact that there is no longer a need to consume raw meat and huge quantities of animal fats; and due to the fact that the physical machine is no longer submitted to an excessive activity as a result of less emotional and mental demands on it, the nature of human needs has shifted toward the realm of more elevated expressions, thus altering human physiology. On the other hand, from the physiological impulses in the area of sex that becomes perverted as a result of the vulgarity to which it has been submitted, disturbances arise in the realm of behavior that create a negative responsibility for the individual, eventually demanding appropriate and inevitable reparations.

The reason behind it is that the evolutionary process leads the physiological individual to a phase of psychological accomplishments, where psychical life prevails over physical life, expanding human aspirations in connection with personal development as humans journey in the direction of immortality.

Consequently, genetic experiments to alter and beautify the organic structure are no more than speculation based, essentially, on the very constitution of the individual, attempting, however, to copy the splendid form designed by the Divinity, but without spiritual correspondence.

The phenomenon of cloning occurs in nature. As is the case, for example, among decapod crustaceans, brachyurous types like crabs and portunid crabs, which, upon losing a leg, it is automatically replaced by the cells that remain and proceed to recreate the amputated limb. This occurrence is also common among other animals such as urodelans and gekkonids, that is, the salamander and the lizard, respectively, whose amputated limbs and tails also grow back, confirming the presence of the biological organizing model.

Therefore, having been invited to cooperate in the beautification of the form, eugenics may establish some guidelines to sculpt the form by acting on the cells; however, without the essential contribution of the agent for transformation, which is the Spirit, it runs the risk of creating monstrous forms causing great harm to the very human being.

Researchers in the field of genetic engineering have dreamed of nothing else, fascinated as they are with improving the form and with the anxious search to find other immediate solutions to some problems —existential challenges— which they expect to solve with human cloning.

Dazzled by the discoveries of the hologram —which always reproduces the whole in any one of its parts— they plan to use the same mechanism to create beings by asexual means, initiating the process by extracting cells from another being that are electronically implanted into the nucleus of a non-fertilized egg, and later transplanted into living organisms that allow them to develop.

Supposedly, successful experiments would have been made in labs with the duplication of zygotes, which were forbidden to continue, such as was the case with sheep that, in the beginning, turned up to be veritable aberrations until achieving success with Dolly and monkeys.

According to their conclusion, this resource would allow for the creation of armies of fighters insensitive to pain because they have no soul; bodies could be stored in special warehouses to supply replacement parts for people whose own body parts have become compromised either by normal wear and tear or abuse; especially programmed intellectuals could be created to solve the many complex, enigmatic, and intricate problems in connection with the cosmos and life; body parts seen as unnecessary for life could be eliminated, etc. —always taking intentionally pre-selected models as reference.

Likewise, by using the semen of geniuses, they could reproduce artists, scientists, philosophers, and abnegated missionaries; or by using the semen of compulsive psychopathic criminals they could reproduce equivalent individuals programmed for war. Ultimately, these scientists would convert their scientific aspirations into unpredictable nightmares, due to the possibility of producing biological monsters that will never have discernment, feelings, and mental activity – slaves that they would be to automatisms that would never become a reality because they cannot complete the life cycle.

The unawareness or deliberate ignorance of these investigators with regards to the Spirit, their high degree of intellectual arrogance, and their distraction in relation to Divine causality lead them to believe that they are in a position to create other beings that would no longer follow the course of nature; beings exclusively driven by their passions in search of nonstop pleasure; beings entirely capable of escaping the inevitable and equally biological phenomenon of death –something no one can escape– for however long a life in the body may be, its constitution is in itself fragile, given the nature of Earth's fluids[9], which support and compose it.

---

9. Fluids: *"So, are the two general elements in the universe: matter and spirit?"* "Yes, and over everything is God, the Creator and author of all. These three elements comprise the principle of all that exists – they are the universal trinity. However, to the element of matter must be added the universal fluid, which plays an intermediary role between spirit and matter per se, since matter is too dense for spirit to act upon it directly. Although from a certain point of view this fluid may be regarded as part of the material element, it differs from it due to special properties. If it were simply matter, there would be no reason for spirit not to be matter too. It is placed between spirit and matter; it is a fluid, just as matter is matter. In its countless combinations with matter, and under the direction of spirit, it is capable of producing an infinite variety of things about which you still know very, very little. By being the agent upon which spirit acts, this universal, primitive or elementary fluid is the principle without which matter would forever remain in a

The cloning of human beings has no chance of becoming a reality because intelligent life cannot be replicated without the thinking agent responsible for charting the course of progress, which —as mandated by life— starts out as *simple and ignorant*, gradually acquiring experience as it reincarnates and develops its incomparable potential waiting for an opportunity to be realized.

Every attempt on the part of scientific investigation to improve the human condition and life in its myriad expressions —inside and outside the planet— is worthy of respect and investment. It falls to researchers, however, to bow before the grandeur of the cosmos and to question the extent of the rights they attribute to themselves, especially those in connection with *correcting* the Natural Law, in whole or in part.

The contribution of Medicine to improve the physical and mental life of individuals is undeniable. It has extended the physical existence as the body becomes more resilient to microbial, bacterial, and viral infections. It corrects certain anomalies thanks to the use of hormones and surgical procedures. It has dialed down pain considerably as it has lost its initial raw quality to become more compatible with an individual's moral strength. It understands human problems and behavioral conflicts. It employs more humane ways

---

state of dispersion; it would never acquire the properties given to it by gravitation."

"Might this fluid be what we call electricity?" "We have stated that it is capable of countless combinations. What you call the electric and magnetic fluids are both modifications of the one universal fluid. Properly speaking, this fluid is a more-perfect and subtler matter that may be considered as independent." See Question 27, *The Spirits' Book* by Allan Kardec (International Spiritist Council, 4th Edition, Revised (2010)). – Tr.

in the treatment of mental insanity more in keeping with human dignity.

The same is true of other scientific disciplines that have transformed the face of the planet by converting swamps into gardens; deserts into farms; building bridges over the abyss; lighting up the world; facilitating communications; bringing higher speeds, more comfort, and hope to benefit all individuals who are in the world working on their own growth thanks to the phenomenon of reincarnation.

All these accomplishments have required a great deal of sacrifice, which a few political pawns and arbitrary public officials of some nations –still stuck at the lower levels of their moral development– have converted into means to materialize their despicable interests, mainly as they fight to impose the vain ascendancy of so-called superior races, of dominating peoples that foment wars and slavery using these unparalleled achievements conducive to progress but which, at their hands, become instruments of consternation and crime.

The intermittent threat of biological weapons and lethal gases hovers frightfully above society –alongside the stockpile of nuclear weapons capable of destroying the planet many times over, reducing it to stardust– because it has not yet been possible to establish ethics on par with the success in the labs; ethics capable of curtailing abuses and restraining atrocious experiments in animals and humans, through which they pursue their subaltern and sordid agenda.

But even if such ethics were, in fact, to be established, then the major issue of compliance would arise, as humanity's worst offenders have never submitted to any controlling measures on the part of other countries –including today's international organizations– or peace agreements, for that matter, signed amidst handshakes and smiles though rarely respected.

This folly drives many genetics' enthusiasts crazy, encouraging them to pursue their unsound ambitions to program a future society of clones: structurally sound specimens, yet without morals or emotions; specimens designed for pleasure as if that were the only motivation for the planetary existence, a life devoid of psychological significance.

Very recently, the Nazis sought to eliminate people with disabilities from their race and destroyed other races, while pursuing their deranged dream of planetary domination. They never considered the passing of their enthusiasts, whose lives and momentary insanity were ultimately snatched by death, teaching a harsh lesson: madness, however prolonged, always claims the life of the host.

Very soon, the governments of the earth will impose limits on macabre research and life-threatening testing, creating bioethical parameters for genetics and science in general giving rise to an existential philosophy based on respect for nature and its inhabitants; a prelude to what will be a New Era of love and peace for all, as announced by Jesus since the days of His ministry among the people of the earth.

11
ORGAN TRANSPLANTS

The horror associated with the inevitable phenomenon of death has driven humans to look for mechanisms —some daring, others pathetic— through which they think they can cheat this biological certainty, whether by using scientific resources to prolong the longevity of the cells and bring about the automatic repair of damaged organs, or by escaping into neurotic disorders.

Scared by the burden that purifying diseases entail, individuals resort to euthanasia, thinking they can avoid pain, or to suicide, in a vain attempt to take an absurd plunge *into the river of absolute oblivion.*

Usually deluded regarding the transitory nature of the cellular archipelago they inhabit, humans become alienated from that reality, anesthetizing their discernment and believing to be free from a future separation from their physical form.

Thankfully, medicine has concluded that real death is determined by the cessation of brainstem activity, and no longer by the mere apparent death of the neurons in the brain.

From time to time, *brain-dead* patients on life support have awakened, demonstrating the presence of an oxygen supply that kept the neurons alive, which allowed these patients to regain conscience and seemingly disrupted physiological functions.

This critical realization led to more in-depth studies and careful observation regarding biological life and its cessation, offering the possibility of new conclusions in this regard, which have allowed for a more dependable definition of the phenomenon of death.

As long as the Spirit remains linked to the body, there will be signs of life, even in the presence of many compromised organs.

A heart that no longer beats and the consequent destruction of the brainstem is what characterizes the separation of the soul from its material envelope, an occurrence that brings about the death of the body.

Thanks to their countless achievements in the realm of knowledge and sentiments, men and women deserve to have their suffering diminished, thus evolving through the inestimable resources of love that is the generating source of life and happiness.

The inevitability of progress has helped humans find the most efficacious means to reach this coveted goal: freedom from suffering.

On account of this effort, as science and technology multiplied their tools to improve our lives, they also enabled the lessening of many sufferings, the complete overcoming of some, and have ended terrible scourges that periodically caused the destruction of millions of lives. At the same time, these conquests have extended the duration of useful life on the planet, providing human beings with more valuable opportunities to use their reincarnation wisely.

With physical pain slowly being banished from the earth and with moral afflictions diminished, it falls to their inhabitants to make profound changes in their ethical and spiritual behavior, so that their conduct will not generate new negative responsibility, different purifying processes, or unknown and devastating diseases as it is still the case.

Usually, when a physical journey ends without a real moral transformation, sequelae contributes to the arising of future warnings through pain, which is Life's natural resource to promote the unstoppable course of evolution.

That way, scientific progress developed the technique for organ transplantation, affording many patients the possibility to bounce back from disease and the effects of natural wear and tear.

A real blessing, organ transplantation prolongs the physical existence; it is a life *extension* thanks to which the Spirit may remain on its physical journey. Life in the body, after all, is a means to arrive at plenitude, which is life in itself, exuberant and real.

People who willingly donate their useful organs with the intent of benefiting their sick brothers and sisters are making a high moral caliber donation, thereby practicing charity in the truest sense by diminishing suffering on the earth.

Organ recipients, in turn –having had the karmic causes behind their suffering attenuated– already deserve such a divine concession. Their physical existence has been extended so they may right their wrongs through the good they do as they improve the living conditions on the planet.

Unsuccessful transplantations are very much a part of the patient's program, as determined by the still prevailing *Law of Cause and Effect*, which prevents the patient from regaining health at the present time. In no way does this mean that the technique is inappropriate or should be disqualified.

The process of organ transplantation could suffer the obsessive interference of a rebellious donor, who was not consulted before the transplant, and is still connected to the physical remains. This will only happen, however, if the recipient is still in debt and if there is attunement between the donor and the recipient, as a result of an inferior psychical condition predominating in both.

Therefore, rejection also happens as a demerit of the beneficiary, whose perispirit did not restructure the received organ, adapting it to his or her needs. Consequently, the perispirit produces reactive substances that expel the *foreign body,* which it does not recognize as its own.

No one in the world is condemned to suffering without reprieve. Love is always the soothing balm within reach for those willing to apply it. Even the most hardened individuals, when they change their mental and emotional disposition attempting to break the oppressive shackles of cruelty or vice, experience the immediate benefits of the vibrations of the good always within their reach.

The Divinity, in turn, bearing witness to human effort on behalf of progress and overcoming pain determines that, from time to time, missionaries of love, wisdom, science, and the arts, take the plunge into the dense layers of the earth's psychosphere[10] to improve the environmental and evolutionary conditions of its inhabitants.

----

10. Psychosphere: Psychical environment. A word used in Spiritism to describe a field created by electromagnetic emissions enwrapping the entire human being, whether incarnate or discarnate. It reveals not only the being's evolutionary reality and psychical characteristics, but also its current emotional and physical conditions. (See more in *Mechanisms of Mediumship,* by Spirit Author Andre Luiz, psychographed by Chico Xavier, Ch. 4). - Tr.

Given this investment on the part of the Divine Love, it falls to human beings to meet the requirements that confer dignity and respectability to their work, without drifting off course toward shameful and despicable interests led by inconsequent and unscrupulous individuals.

The indiscriminate sale of organs is one such example that opens the door to an ignominious business notorious for instigating heinous crimes that should horrify humanity. Humankind must abhor this type of commerce.

Such practices favor the rich and bypass the poor; they foster discrimination because they choose people based on their material assets instead of the significance of their lives.

It also creates the conditions for the hasty removal of organs before real death has occurred −the death of the brainstem− under false pretenses in connection with the death of the brain... Besides, it encourages criminal organizations to kidnap children and homeless individuals without identification to take their organs for this nefarious trade. Such actions may very well respond for terrible future obsessions in which the victims −who were never consulted about the transplant− claim the organs taken without their consent or seek revenge for having suffered the excruciating pain of the surgeries to which they were submitted after the homicide they were powerless to prevent.

There is an urgent need for the establishment of bioethics with regards to organ transplantations as well as for a clear and conscientious preparation of the donors. Donors must always be volunteers, for a mandatory act would leave them at the mercy of unprincipled legislators exclusively preoccupied with their own interests, far removed from the spiritual knowledge that is the basis for life.

The body is a patrimony received from God meant to serve as a vehicle for the Spirit through its multifarious reincarnations, as it leaves the shadows to conquer the light. Deserving of all our respect and reverence, it is an instrument of light that ignorance or the persistence in evil transforms into shadows or a miasma storehouse causing its own affliction.

Every investment of love on behalf of the body produces tenuous vibrations that refine and energize its components, generating forces that bring about balance and promote strength.

When individuals become aware of their own immortality and understand the value of donating their organs –precious organs that have served them so well and are now facing decomposition– to other individuals in order to diminish suffering and save lives, they will see organ donation as an honorable way to achieve inner growth.

Eyes, which have seen beauty, will restore sight to someone stumbling in the dark; kidneys, which have filtered the blood of life, will spare someone the serious risks associated with dialysis; healthy skin will replace torn or burnt skin... Hearts, lungs, livers, and glands, which science can use at the appropriate time, will be exceptional gifts for humankind – provided that donors were really dead.

Scientific advances will reach that point and go well beyond, as is already the case with microsurgery for the brain and other similar procedures that extend the physical existence to speed up the process of spiritual evolution.

Once the organ has been transplanted into the recipient's body, the recipient's perispirit automatically begins to influence the new organ by *adapting* it to its needs. For this reason, the patient must undergo an urgent moral transformation for the better so that the course of its trials may be altered, generating new causes that allow for happiness, which, perhaps, the patient does not yet deserve.

As a Spirit thinks and acts, it is continuously changing its physical existence, for as it keeps generating causes, it will eventually experience their inevitable effects.

Organ transplantation —when performed for the enhancement of human life and under the auspices of bioethics anchored on the Law of Love— is a major step for humanity in its journey toward a better future, even if death, which awaits everyone, continues to be the inevitable process of liberation from the body to live a spiritual existence, the true and eternal one.

12
CRYOPRESERVATION OF HUMAN BEINGS

The high-level technological advancement achieved by humans is yet to convince them about the fragility and transient nature of the bodies they use during the physical journey.

Wishing for the eternal life of the physical body, they consistently fail to realize that this is, in fact, already the case, albeit on other levels –causal, immanent levels– such as the Higher Self or the Spirit, that traveler of a thousand journeys.

Wanting to beat death, they come up with mechanisms to remain in the physical body, trying to dodge the degenerative factors inherent to its constitution. Despite recognizing the inevitability of the disorder brought about by the phenomenon of entropy –derived from the consumption of energy– which reverts material organizations to chaos as they move, they continue to delude themselves with an indefinite permanence in the cellular universe.

In order to remain in the envelope of flesh and without any pain whatsoever, they continue to search for the fountain of eternal youth, the preservation of the body, or its perpetuation, dreaming of the day when they will achieve success.

A spiritual perspective of reality completely changes that intellectual stance, demonstrating that humans are beings made for eternity, for eternal youth, for well- being, and for health. This, however, happens in another dimension, since the earth —on account of its very constitution— is subject to permanent changes as it refines and changes its intrinsic structure. It is true that the earth is not a paradise, but it is not a *valley of tears* either —as affirmed by old doctrines within the orthodox faith. It is a school that also progresses as its students improve and begin to require more specific resources for their development. Nonetheless, that day will come, no doubt, but outside the material organization, which is always temporary because it is a tool life uses to attain the essential goal: a state of plenitude.

Therefore, health and disease are the binomial expression of the existential mechanism, which works harmoniously for the transformation and improvement of spiritual values that are the essence of the very human being.

So, it is natural that, periodically, humanity is swept by challenging diseases that become a heavy burden to bear, as well as a motivation to search for new resources to contribute to its eradication, or at least to lessen the suffering.

Consequently, it is good to conduct continuous research; to work for the renewal of existential parameters; to endeavor to change concepts and behaviors, which may somehow contribute to making our stay on the earth more harmonious. However, expecting to apply these achievements in the elimination of disease is, for the time being, pointless just as attempting to stop biological death is entirely impossible.

The aging and the decaying of the cells, with their consequent decomposition and substitution by other cells is an inescapable mandate to which the body is subject, until such time when this process of renewal is no longer viable and, as a result, the whole structure disintegrates. This moment can be delayed for some time by having a sound moral and mental behavior and by engaging in activities that foster inner balance; however, the irreversible process of birth-death within biological parameters can never be stopped.

At present, scientists study the possibility of using cryogenics on patients with diseases for which there is no known palliative care or ways to prevent their death. This effort, however, although respectable, has no chances to succeed.

The death of a person is not just caused by the body's inability to keep the person alive, or by internal damage precipitated by degenerative diseases or violent outcomes. The death of a person is also caused by the disengagement of the Spirit from its nuclei of energy preservation –which give sustenance to matter– or by the Spirit's expulsion in sudden and traumatic circumstances. Once these bonds are broken, bringing the patient back to life is completely impossible because the process of molecular disorganization soon begins, and, without the presence of the vital agent, matter decomposes and immediately transforms, setting its biological fatalism into motion.

On the other hand, by using cryogenic methods to prevent the death of a patient whose disease cannot be cured at present, the agent engages in an act with unforeseeable consequences that deserve examination, albeit a quick one.

There is no guarantee that the patient would awaken around the time science could cure his or her disease, or lessen the severity of the pain. Besides, there is no proof that long-term cryopreservation of a human being may be achieved without causing brain damage or similar damage to other organs.

Furthermore, the presence of recurrent wars decimating lives through the centuries becomes a permanent threat to any long-term human undertaking, as is has frequently been the case.

We would still face the *ghost* of emerging new diseases, something that has happened all throughout history; as soon as a disease is eradicated, another even more terrible one takes its place. This is so because human beings have not yet learned to overcome the factors that generate problems for their physical and mental health.

We could also add various questions of a psychological nature, such as: What would be the meaning of a person's existence feeling like a total stranger in a group with which he or she has absolutely nothing in common? How would we face ourselves after realizing that we are selfish and have ran away from reality to achieve a goal that left us empty-handed and emotionally fragile? How would we emotionally cope with the absence of loved ones currently in another dimension? How would we deal with entirely new knowledge and habits completely different from what we had before? How would we adapt to that new world, which will have undergone innumerable changes since the time we allowed ourselves to undergo cryopreservation?

We could ask other questions for which there are no reassuring answers either, such as: How would we manage our current conflicts in a different emotional state and in completely unforeseeable circumstances? How would our immunological system react in the face of society's diseases at the time?

Beside many intriguing questions, we could still die in accidents, from emotional and traumatic shocks, from unexpected anguish, or even diseases spreading at the time.

The lack of a vision about God in the hearts and minds of the scientists investigating the phenomena of life is what leads them to the mistaken belief that the body and its components are the only material that makes existence possible, and therefore must be used hedonistically in the search for sensual and immediate pleasure.

Cryogenics, however, is meant to play an important role in product preservation. This includes cryopreservation of body parts for future transplants and sperm banks for responsible motherhood, in cases when physical factors prevent pregnancy by conventional means and Divine Mercy has altered the person's debits –the reason behind the impediment– so that love may grant the sublime wish.

Therefore, no one can devise ways to stop human beings from dying or fool the mechanisms to atone for grave mistakes dating to past lives. The Law of Life sees that the offender is always followed by the shadow of his or her mistake until such time when love cancels out the gravity of the responsibility, opening the door to self-realization, to a peaceful conscience, and to resume the march along the path of progress.

13
DISTURBING EUGENICS

According to lexicographers, *eugenics is the science that studies the best conditions to reproduce and improve the human race.*

There are two ways to achieve this goal: a) obstructing the reproduction of defective genes –negative eugenics; b) encouraging the reproduction of healthy genes that can produce superior bodies –positive eugenics.

The knowledge regarding these possibilities and their subsequent implementation are considered to be valuable resources to produce healthy individuals with a perfect biology, at once creating a race that is beautiful, harmonious, and always susceptible of further improvement.

This *fantastic dream* would help *construct* in the lab ideal beings resistant to diseases, aging and deterioration, as if they were working on a clump of cells submissive to the whims of their new architects, catering to all their passions in the frantic quest for beauty and perfection, albeit according to the mental parameters of their *creators*.

Life and the human race would become a toy at the hands of researchers. By acting on some DNA molecules, they could transform the phenomenon of the existential being into a mere technical job of genetic engineering.

The concept of perfection, however, is relative. What seems chaotic, ugly, or deficient to some, seems harmonious and beautiful to others —something that would pose a significant problem at the time of choosing the ideal biotype.

In the various ethnicities, different characteristics and morphological constitutions present special beauty types – according to the taste of the members within the same ethnic group.

The selection of a form to be considered as the model —as dreamed by the Nazis with the pure Aryan race– failed because it did not present any superiority when compared to others, culminating in the fall of the III Reich.

A stoic and bellicose appearance, haughtiness and arrogance have more to do with a Spirit's pride than with the genetic constitution of the Aryan race, for if such individuals indeed had that appearance, many others were found to have disabilities and limitations, suffering from physical and mental issues identical to the ones suffered by many individuals of other ethnicities.

In this case, eugenics was used in an opprobrious way to eliminate the weak and preserve the strong. Because they could not reach the integral being —the Spirit– even those with physical vigor and elegance according to European parameters, succumbed to despair, anguish, loneliness, and psychological conflicts, whose roots are found in the conscience, in what happened before the current physical existence.

The body will always reflect each being's moral triumphs or defeats.

Molded by the perispirit —which obeys the determinations of the Spirit's evolution– it is only by working on the causes that real results may be obtained; this can never be done in the lab.

Attempts at enhancing the quality of plants and some animals may be met with success by using eugenic methods to achieve better preservation, modification of the form, insect resistance, muscular development, and weight gain –so much in vogue these days– even though the harm that the indiscriminate use of hormones, mainly in poultry but also in other animals, has been causing to human health cannot be predicted or estimated.

The disorderly quest to enhance living beings for the marketplace has presented problems that remain unknown to the general public, but end up affecting the behavior and the overall harmony of the body.

From a different angle, eugenics plans to counsel couples with genetic disorders to avoid having children, in an effort to avoid procreating future generations of individuals with deficiencies.

Specialists in the field of eugenics want to identify fetuses that present abnormalities to propose the termination of the pregnancy. They want to stop the birth of babies born with diseases and deficiencies of any kind, in a grotesque attempt to fool the Divine Laws.

Other recommendations are put forth in a repressive way, such as avoiding unions between members of the same family –including cousins– given the chances of having children with serious genetic diseases, as well as having women no longer procreate after the age of 35 –and particularly after 40– given the high probability of conceiving children with severe conditions such as Down Syndrome, among others, at that stage in life.

Breakthroughs in the field of genetics, however, have been allowing women over 50 –many of them grandmothers already– to conceive perfectly healthy babies with relative success.

In that light, eugenics would enable the emergence of an ideal race, made of especially perfect beings, as if it were feasible to avoid what has been programmed by the Law of Cause and Effect.

If it were possible to improve the genetic constitution and established difficult events –which are necessary for the Spirit– suffering would later appear in the form of accidents or unpredictable illnesses, singling out individuals with debts who can neither escape from themselves nor from the equanimity of Divine Justice. Therefore, only by living an honorable existence can the Spirit obtain a healthy body as the natural outcome of its achievements. In turn, this will produce races in which abnormalities and deficiencies no longer predominate, as these are mechanisms of rehabilitation and moral improvement.

True eugenics, the only one with the means to interfere in the molecules of the DNA to produce harmonious and beautiful bodies, originates in the eternal Spirit, the real builder of the vehicle through which it manifests on the earth. So, it falls to the Spirit to have a better incarnation in keeping with legal and moral parameters.

Even if human laws adopt criminal eugenic methods to eliminate the weak and individuals with deficiencies – preventing them from multiplying in the name of a superior race– humanity will regrettably face a terrible ethical problem bound to weigh very heavily on its shoulders.

The authentic and meaningful superiority that stands out in human beings does not come from belonging to a particular race or social condition, that is to say, from a physical origin. It derives from an individual's moral values and intellectual achievements applied on behalf of the good and human progress. That is what constitutes a true aristocracy, but of a spiritual nature.

The improvement of races and the human body will come as a result of the Law of Progress –as has been the case from the start– which through millennia has shown very significant changes for the better in connection with the form as well as its resistance to diseases and degenerative processes. This is the product of natural selection, but it is also no less the fruit of the Spirit's moral development along its successive incarnations, as it progressively builds more balanced vessels better suited for its inner growth.

Without intending to put up obstacles to the progress of research and development in the different fields of knowledge, we should never forget that science without God brutalizes human beings and makes them arrogant, delusional and sometimes despicable.

An understanding of the order and the balance ruling the cosmos –having the Creator as their foundation– make honorable and ethical scientific work possible, helping human beings with their intellectual, moral, and spiritual development as they strive to attain complete realization as collaborators in the Divine Works.

14
SEX CHANGE

The constitution of organic beings derives from their evolutionary needs, which are molded by the perispirit as the biological organizing model.

Bringing the evolutionary mechanisms already imprinted on the subtle recesses of its intimate structure, the perispirit molds –at the time of conception– the body that the Spirit will use during its human journey, to improve its character and rectify past life mistakes.

Working on the genetic codes of the DNA, the perispirit exerts its action on the molecules that supply the cells, which in turn program the form, while the Spirit is responsible for producing emotional phenomena and psychical faculties.

Therefore, the Spirit is the heir to its own legacy, promoting the means for inner growth through experiences that take place in the female as well as the male sexual polarity.

Considering the very important purpose of the genetic apparatus –responsible for reproduction– it is a repository of special hormones that work in conjunction with hormones from the other endocrine glands so that physical, emotional, and intellectual balance may be expressed naturally, without trauma or dysfunction derived from problems yet to be solved.

When expressed in moderation, the libido promotes creativity and productivity in the individual, as the natural, ancestral outcome of the very long instinctual phase whose characteristics remain dominant.

Any disruption in the libido promptly generates neurotic and behavioral disturbances that severely affect the process of reincarnation, given their strong connection.

This powerful driving energy requires careful guidance to produce harmonious phenomena that stimulate order and ennobling realization; otherwise, its force bursts like a dam leaving a trail of destruction behind.

The appropriate use of the sexual function –an agreement between a person's psychology and physiology– generates well-being and promotes spiritual growth, without forging bonds with the instinctual phase from the past and perverse and addicted *entities* connected with it.

Abstinence, when such energy is shaped and converted into inspiration and an acting force to achieve ideals of beauty, culture, and personal sacrifice, it also provides balance and empathy, for what matters is the harnessing of its psychical elements, which are produced to remain in constant motion.

Consequently, it is of fundamental importance that the incarnate Spirit is entirely identified with its sexual anatomy, maintaining its psychological motivations in consonance as well.

When it is the other way around –the person's emotions clash with the person's anatomy– we have a Spirit in rehabilitation. Thus, the need for discipline, not consenting with an inappropriate use that would generate more severe consequences for the future.

For this reason, it is of vital importance that parents respect the sex of their children, refraining from *interfering* psychically during the gestational process, when the zygote begins to define its future form in consonance with the karmic map of the reincarnating Spirit.

It is natural to prefer this or that gender for a loved one; however, this desire should not be so preponderant that, when it turns out to be different from one's wishes, one's love may be negatively impacted. Likewise, the lack of vigilance that can cause a mother to choose and impose her wish on the developing being could contribute to altering its molecular constitution, as it attends to her wish through psychokinetic mechanisms. At any rate, because it is not part of the Spirit's evolutionary program, said *change* could cause emotional and behavioral problems.

The genetic structure that elaborates the body is made up of powerful elements —albeit subtle— that obey the energy plan acting upon it. Consequently, the mind of the reincarnating Spirit —consciously or not— as well as the minds of the parents significantly interfere in the construction of the Spirit's anatomy by acting directly on the genes and their chromosomes —if the desire should become strong and continuous. Such psychical action can alter the purines and pyrimidines pairs in the DNA structure, changing the original program already under development. This is not a rare occurrence. If anything, it happens much more frequently than it has been detected, particularly in instances where the Spirit imprints characteristics that it brings from past existences — suicide, homicide, and accidents— or behaviors that became so deeply ingrained that now emerge in the new form.

Likewise, offspring presenting a different anatomy from the spiritually planned one —in some cases due to the preference of the parents, especially the mother, who psychically *crafted* the anatomy with a continuous and exaggerated desire during pregnancy– have difficulty expressing themselves and experience behavioral disorders, which must be corrected during childhood to prevent them from becoming a problem in adolescence –a time when organs and secondary sexual characteristics reach definition.

A loving and careful guidance restructures the binary expression form-emotion, allowing for a healthy physical existence, without anguish or distress.

This situation could be greatly aggravated when experts in the field of genetic engineering –in their ambitious attempts to try to interfere in people's lives– start reprogramming the sex already under development through the DNA genetic codes, altering the anatomy and the function.

In such cases, the prevailing spiritual program –now suffering the influence of external meddling– gives rise to individuals with complex behavioral problems in that area. These individuals positively needed to have an experience in the original sexual polarity that was later changed. So, finding themselves in a different polarity that is not consonant with their wishes or psychical needs, they develop issues.

There are already innumerable such cases driving individuals to escape through drugs that create dependence, exhaust their strength, and ultimately consume them when they do not commit suicide in a desperate attempt to run away from the conflict that overwhelms and tears them apart, for they believe that their problem has no solution, and therefore there is no reason to go on living.

The question of sexuality is very delicate and profound. It demands serious studies dispensing with the solutions offered by vulgarity –hasty and superficial– that tries to solve conflictive situations by suggesting nonsensical behavior that violates the being's moral structures. As a result, the individual begins to experience psychical disturbances or feelings of self-loathing, despite maintaining an outward appearance of success that is far from having been achieved.

At the moment of conception, the perispirit is attracted by an incomparable force toward the cells that begin to form, automatically impressing upon such cells –by virtue of the power of *The Law of Cause and Effect*– what is necessary for the Spirit to evolve including, no doubt, the sex and its relevant functions.

External meddling altering this shaping process will only cause problems, inflict damages, and generate moral imbalances.

As genetic engineering penetrates into the origins of physical life, it will make a highly valuable contribution, provided that it does not arrogate to itself the presumptuous right to interfere with the higher plans in connection with the realization and construction of the human being.

The body produces the body, which is the heir to many ancestral family traits that suffer the influence of the environment. Only the Spirit produces character, tendencies, moral qualities, intellectual achievements, and destiny.

For this reason, the vain attempt to effect a sex change –during the embryonic period or at any other time during the physical existence– is an act of defiance to the Law of Harmony effective in the Creation, which will cause untold disturbances to the personality and to the person's mental life.

All bodies are deserving of ongoing respect, attention, love, and care because they are the seat of the Spirit, the sanctuary where life unfolds. However, when it comes to the area of sexuality –considering its reproductive functions as well as its powerful and critical hormonal exchanges– individuals are invited to exercise greater vigilance and discipline.

Sexual education through appropriate mental discipline is a challenge in connection with our happiness, a challenge we all face and must overcome.

The shackles of sexual vices have been holding millions of men and women in the rearguard of the passions who, upon reincarnating, will face difficult and challenging problems requiring painful solutions. Unwilling to sacrifice in order to solve said problems, these individuals continue to live in unfortunate and afflictive circumstances.

Any conscientious abuse perpetrated on the body –and particularly in the area of sexuality– generates equivalent damages, which will require appropriate reparations on the part of its perpetrators as they begin to suffer the consequences.

So, when facing any difficulty or having to make crucial decisions requiring resolve, we can always ask Love about the best way to go. That ubiquitous Love, free from the drawbacks of the passions, will answer with superior wisdom, which, if carefully heeded, will provide balance and peace, propelling the Spirit along the right path to reach the goal for which it reincarnated in the first place.

15
MULTIPLE
PERSONALITIES

With the discovery of the subconscious during the decade 1880-90, Prof. Pierre Janet proposed that intellectual mediumistic phenomena could be explained as the result of pathologies that appear as multiple or parasitic personalities. Such personifications would originate in different events that occurred in a person's life –mainly during childhood– when the person had dreams or aspirations that did not materialize in adulthood. Those dreams and ambitions were then archived in the subconscious until the time they finally exteriorized giving the impression of being manifestations of the souls of the dead.

According to the eminent master, in a certain way they would also be the result of states of hysteria –given the tendency, at the time, to label as such everything that was not understood in the area of psychopathologies –which could be evoked, even unconsciously, at which point they would assume a predominant role in the current consciousness.

The daring thesis would be the outcome of research conducted by Dr. Jean Martin Charcot with psychopathic patients –particularly women– at Bicêtre Hospital, in Paris.

With the use of hypnosis, it was possible to cause the irruption of a patient's emotional disturbances, triggering a liberating catharsis for their conflicts and traumas.

Undoubtedly, many unfulfilled aspirations are archived in the recesses of the soul in the layers of the subconscious as well as the unconscious, which can somehow interfere in a person's behavior at different times during the physical existence.

The traumas derived from these unfulfilled aspirations contribute to the emergence of conflicts that emotionally destabilize the patient, appearing from time to time and predominating in the conscious Self as a pathological mechanism of exteriorization.

This point has a logical basis, no doubt, but it does not encompass all the factors in its psychopathogenesis.

There are other factors in the understanding of parasitic or multiple personalities that were not considered, such as the interference of discarnate Spirits through mediumistic processes. In some cases, these interferences can be powerful to the point of producing obsessive states, which are diseases that require a greater investment of in-depth and careful research, analysis, and study on the part of the psychical sciences.

As an eternal being, the Spirit experiences numerous opportunities to develop its capability for self-illumination, given all the valuable treasures offered by the Divinity. Since it does not always know how to behave, the Spirit uses these treasures selfishly, inconsiderately, or foolishly, thus generating difficulties for itself in reincarnations ahead.

In the beginning, the Spirit gets into trouble and returns to make amends, to relearn, gaining discernment meant to guide its free will and lend moderation to its attitudes. Not always listening to the voice of discernment, however, the

Spirit creates disastrous struggles and acquires resources that only perturb it, when it does not create profound animosities or hatreds that can last for centuries, or generate a whole host of painful entanglements that the Spirit must deal with along the process of inner growth.

Many such regrettable follies open the door to resentment and rancor on the part of those who suffered the shameful constriction, the unwarranted treason, or the consequences of the dishonest maneuvers. The victims that do not forgive assume the role of creditors expecting compensations for the damages. To that avail, they establish a connection with the perpetrators through waves of hatred that attract and magnetize them in a painful and disconcerting psychopathological process.

For this reason, spirit obsessions or physical and psychical constrictions on human beings are numerous and, on the rise, as they are a resource for the moral purification of those who disregard the Laws for their own ends.

Naturally, the Divinity does not need for victims to become debt collectors or executioners of their brothers and sisters —even after having suffered multiple abuses— for God has the right mechanisms to deal with each offense, embedded in the conscience of every being. However, the main state of the victim —equally attuned with the one who hurt and harmed it— establishes a psychical and vibrational connection that facilitates an interference in the mental *force fields,* giving rise to the parasitic mechanisms of painful spirit persecutions.

This is one of the most painful chapters in the realm of spiritual exchanges because, while the former offender expunges, its former victim —even without knowing— assumes the role it fights against. By acting as judge and creditor, it becomes a perpetrator and an unfair avenger.

Only the Cosmic Consciousness, in its justice and wisdom, has the proper means to heal dysfunctional relationships, cancel past irregularities, and substitute good done at a future date for past damages.

Having in-depth knowledge about the past of both adversaries –victim and perpetrator– it fairly and wisely evaluates the factors that caused the problem, the circumstances in which it took place, and the corresponding liability, resorting to the tools that purify through love, benevolence, charity, and forgiveness to rebuild the path to fraternity and make everyone into friends, helping them understand that making mistakes is an inevitable experience of the process of evolution.

That being said, many multiple personality cases that appear in psychopathologies are the presence of spirits interfering with the behavior of human beings, requiring the appropriate therapy to awaken their consciences and to show them that they are treading the wrong path at a considerable expense to themselves.

This is not easy to do, just as nothing that is noble or honorable ever is. Everything in life poses a significant challenge that demands investment concerning responsibility and work in order to reach the goal. However, patience born out of compassion for the oppressor as well as uplifting guidance for the oppressed –in addition to other contributions– manage to change the landscape and sometimes set the combatants free from one another and the insanity of hatred.

Those who feel let down and want to settle the score plug themselves into their targets using receptacles found in the very individual. For this reason, if there is no real change in the patients' intentions, a vibrational modification in their mental and moral life, they are predisposed to the negative interference, to the presence of the *intrusive personality* that acts through them, assuming control of their body and mind according to the severity of the crime that identifies and binds them together.

Simultaneously, there could also be —as a propitious factor to the presence of parasitic personalities— undiluted reminiscences from the unconscious, where past existences are stored, particularly those characterized by the prevalence of intense experiences that continue to percolate from the deep foundation and deposits, assuming control of the current Self.

Almost always, they are memories related to very drastic behavior that became firmly imprinted in the recesses of the soul and now automatically reemerge, overrunning our current state of lucidity and commanding present-day conduct.

Overbearing impressions and strong behaviors lived in the past continue to dictate causing the psyche to lose control. Its predominance leads men and women to very painful experiences, and to sexual and emotional conflicts.

The history of every life is engraved in the very being, which is tied to every action and fact that predominated in its past existences. *Today* is the continuation of *yesterday,* which is to be continued by *tomorrow.* In its relativity, after all, time is immutable. All individuals and all things pass through it carrying the load of their respective realizations.

The chapter of multiple or parasitic personalities is very delicate and complex due to the indestructibility of life, the immortality of the soul, and the exchanges that exist among all living beings, particularly among Spirits —which everyone is— despite the different evolutionary stages.

Jesus, the psychotherapist par excellence, wisely and solicitously warned: *Do not do to others what you would not have them do to you*, demonstrating that we will reap what we sow.

Integral health, therefore, will always be the result of a guiltless conscience, a tender heart, and a balanced behavior.

16
DEATH AND REBIRTH

The integral being is a traveler of Eternity, progressing step-by-step, in such a way that the experiences lived on each journey in the flesh set up the evolutionary mechanisms for the next journey, enabling endless development.

Since its creation, the being goes through incessant transformations that make it bloom, breaking out of its prison, and growing in search of its eternal destination –relative perfection– which it cannot yet foresee as it lacks resources and aptitudes for such a thorough understanding.

Every conquest is incontestably etched in the most delicate weavings of its subtle organization –the perispirit– as the shaping device that programs future behaviors for the process of moral progress in the material realm. Composed of specific and *molding* energy, this intermediary body is in charge of registering all moral and mental occurrences that will consubstantiate the future form, the mechanism of rehabilitation, as well as the instrument for the conversion of values necessary for its own purification.

Based on the being's behavior during the physical existence, the processes for its liberation through the action of death –an occurrence that is much more important than it may seem to the less careful observer– are, in a certain way, being delineated.

As we live, so we die. Thoughts and actions are implacable weavers responsible for the final detachment that liberates de Spirit from the body.

Consequently, the terminal event responsible for a person's passing is the result of the entire process lived during the physical stage. Each person experiences a process of liberation according to how they acted while incarnate, which in turn becomes their future existential programs.

A violent passing not only causes great perturbation but can also be the reason for a difficult future process of corporeal rebirth.

A carefully planned suicide causes profound traumas resulting in an upcoming pain-filled reincarnation, beginning with a pregnancy ridden with numerous complications before and during the delivery, when it does not fail in very painful circumstances. Death by hanging, for example, results in a rebirth under the constriction of the umbilical cord causing severe asphyxia to the baby. Death by poisoning determines a new beginning with irrecoverable brain damage caused by anoxia. Death by drowning determines the rupture of the placenta before delivery. A body destroyed by someone who jumped form great heights, threw himself or herself under a heavy vehicle, or engaged in self-inflected mutilations determines a return in an inadequate position from which there is no release, or with congenital abnormalities such as a deformed body and other severe anomalies.

The troublesome rebirth does not impede but is rather related to the existence that will be marked by the harmful effects of the act of self-destruction, which is always a shameful and cruel mechanism for a Spirit to force its way out of matter. Thus, no one can evade their duties with impunity, for we return to find them, at a later time, more complex and demanding than before.

Suicide answers for the degenerative processes that many individuals suffer from while on the earthly journey, as they face the consequences of such an insane act, such a rebellion against the Sovereign Laws.

The disastrous act by which the transgressor wishes to run away from his or her conscience becomes even more affixed, imposing the repetition of the phenomenon of death in order to learn to respect the conditions imposed by life.

On the other hand, when the departure from the earth is caused by accidents that cause a great deal of terror, such events can negatively affect the future return to the material realm. The caustic suffering they cause will reflect as incessant afflictions during the upcoming incarnation, which will be marked by suffering and distressing conflicts.

Human beings are always sowing and reaping within a determinism they cannot escape, for it is the sole and salutary means to develop all the values lying dormant within.

Death and rebirth are processes that complete one another because they are part of the same phenomenon of life. Since the Spirit is the determining factor in its own illuminative experience, everything it elaborates in the mind and materializes, or not, becomes its personal patrimony, acquiring even greater significance when it is translated into action.

A thought is a powerful vehicle, not only for communication and personal growth but also as a strong energy moving in the universe. It is a co-creational force that the Spirit possesses to ascend from the lowest stages to the heights of progress. For this reason, it must be very well directed, since every mental wave emission elicits an equivalent attunement, meant to become a fortunate or an unfortunate venture as the result of its intrinsic content.

Birthmarks —more than the outcome of genetic factors— are signals programmed by the Spirit in connection with how its last passing occurred, and which are imprinted in the DNA codes, as is also the case with easy, complicated or unsuccessful deliveries.

As the old saying goes: *we die as we have lived*. We may add that we will begin again as we have died.

17

SURVIVAL AND SPIRIT COMMUNICATION

In the course of human beings' psychological and anthropological evolutionary process, spiritual exchanges stand out, thoroughly demonstrating the survival of the Spirit to the biological phenomenon of cellular disjuncture.

Responsible for acquiring the organic implements it needs to evolve, the eternal being molds, during each journey to which it submits, the appropriate equipment for the blossoming of its inherent faculties.

Before humans became aware of this mechanism, death always seemed to be the cessation of the principle of life, apparently plunging reality into the annihilation of forms.

The fear of total annihilation, the lack of discernment between reality and myth, and the predominance of the instinct of self-preservation drove primitive men and women to observe the brutal rupture of life when death's overwhelming force appeared. With no capacity to discriminate or to think logically –reacting rather than acting rationally– the pain over the loss of a loved one became unbearable and brutal.

In said instances, in the silence of the caves where they sought shelter, primitive men and women were visited by the very beings their eyes saw decomposing in mortuary silence. So, inevitably, the presence of those who returned attempting to communicate left a terrifying impression on their souls.

Prior to that, however, during the Paleolithic period, *cult stones* were the rudimentary way by which people expressed their emerging beliefs. They attempted to represent the human image on fragments of rock where they painted themselves with crude and rough lines —albeit schematically. Sometime later, as human thought evolved, people started sculpting on mud, bone, wood, and stone with better-defined lines, arranging their work around the bonfires where they warmed up.

That was the beginning of shamanic practices and the first sensitives appeared, who did not realize that they were the instruments for the phenomena, which began to express through movement with the *falling stones*.

There was a huge gap between the first visual manifestations and making palpable contact, during which the first communications allowing for the exchanges between the two spheres of life took place, building the bridge of mediumship to that avail.

On the deteriorated walls of the caves where they hid, illuminated by crackling flames, forms appeared. At first, they were vague and imprecise but, over time, they began to condense until they became the ghosts of the disappeared ancestors, who insisted on lingering, despite the horror stamped in the grotesque faces of the humans with whom they wished to communicate.

This phenomenon became so common that its inevitability made it acceptable. At first, people were apprehensive, but in time it became a patrimony of humanity.

The natural and continuous observation of the phenomenon created instruments to make it happen —now out of interest on the part of the visited ones— upon corroborating that it only occurred when certain members of the group were present. The identification of the mechanism that produced the phenomenon led to the selection of those who became its intermediaries — giving rise to the emergence of more sophisticated ways of worship, magic, *witchcraft,* a practice forbidden in all ancestral legislations, which proves its existence— of people endowed with resources that could produce said manifestations.

Human thought, subject to ancient atavisms —mainly the fear of the unknown that people always see as a threat to their security— later evolved to create myths as a way to absorb that reality that it could not understand.

Evolving in a hostile environment —terrifying seismic events, ferocious animals, antagonistic groups, aggressive and devastating diseases, and the lack of adequate nourishment that was as rudimentary as life itself— primitive men and women began to gain inspiration and knowledge from instructions received during said communications with their ancestors.

By way of small, almost insignificant suggestions, the immortals set out to guide humans still in the body, by pointing the way that would facilitate their march, diminishing their pain and helping them face critical challenges. This guidance would later give rise to prophecy, *miraculous* interventions, fanaticism, and a misguided submission to discarnate beings, supposedly left in charge of disciplining and guiding human life —something that continues to be the dominant archetype in many people's minds.

Back then, it was understandable that this phenomenon took place and gained acceptance, for it provided help until individuals acquired reason and judgment. From this point on, people realized that death was only a process of transformation and not one of miraculous sublimation, and therefore they could discern what they should and should not accept in terms of guidelines coming from the spirit world.

Reaching that level of understanding of the legitimacy of life in the two planes of evolutionary existence demanded millennia of learning and observation, until the arrival of Spiritism with its precious arsenal, equally brought forth by the spirit beings that composed it, together with its codifier: Allan Kardec.

From the dark caves illuminated by crackling flames to the sanctuaries erected to that avail was a step; from the silence and the shadows in which the phenomenon happened best to similar man-made structures was also the natural result of observation, multiplying as individuals grew mentally and developed socially, leading up to the inevitable occurrence in which *the dead start guiding the living.*

In the ancient East, whether in sumptuous temples or beneath the stars, communications took place as invocations to the gods –who were none other than Spirits who had earned respect for the work they had done on behalf of the people– willing to listen to human requests, establishing rules, formalities, and dispensing help compatible with the level of understanding of those who sought their advice.

Indeed, not all the Spirits that gave communications were elevated enough to dispense sound advice. Many of them, still attached to the passions they cultivated before their death, returned and imposed their fanciful, violent, and bloodthirsty will, becoming responsible for the despicable influence that obstructed the march of progress for a long time.

Such an occurrence is very understandable, given society's state of consciousness at the time. Emerging from the tribal stage, it was taking its first steps toward what would be the civilization of the future in which, unfortunately, debased passions and unwise habits still predominate, causing regressions and relapses through which it gradually climbs the steps toward progress and freedom.

Eastern and Western historians have left us beautiful pages and captivating accounts of events regarding Spirit exchanges and their beneficial results, for which they were the instruments or were recounted to them by real witnesses. Today, these pages are a resource to emulate in order to have a prosperous existence on the earth, as well as the certainty concerning the continuation of life after the death of the body.

In *The Daemon of Socrates*, Xenophon puts the following information in the mouth of the philosopher: "*This prophetic voice has been heard by me throughout the course of my entire life; it is certainly more authentic than the auguries drawn from the flight or the entrails of the birds: I call it God or Demon. I have communicated to my friends the warnings I have received. And until now, the voice has never affirmed anything that was inexact.*"

And not just Xenophon but also Plutarch, Plato, and other *disciples* have confirmed the communications maintained between the sage and the spirit world.

Attesting to the low evolutionary level of some of the Spirits that communicated, Plutarch makes reference to the incident with Brutus, when the latter is confronted by a Spirit who peremptorily affirmed "I am your bad angel, Brutus, and you will see me near the city of the Philippians" to which the courageous warrior responded "Fine, so I will see you there."

At a later time, mercilessly persecuted by Mark Anthony and Octavian, Cassius and Brutus were defeated in 42 BC, in the fields of Philippi in Macedonia.

Without the moral fortitude to deal with the defeat and incapable of saving the Republic, Brutus threw himself on the tip of a lance, which killed him confirming his *bad angel's* inauspicious omen.

Understanding that the real world is the causal one and the spirit world is where beings originate –and not the other way around– it is easy to comprehend that the proof of immortality comes from the psychical realm and not the physical realm, to awaken consciences that are asleep in the body to the evolutionary objectives to which they are bound.

Having a broader view of reality and living it in plenitude, a Spirit can offer more precise information in connection with the real values and objectives that deserve to be cultivated and pursued, thereby ascribing existential meaning to the physical journey, which then acquires great psychological significance.

Having currently achieved a substantial cultural and scientific magnitude, spiritual exchanges elucidate various occurrences that remained in the shadows in the areas of behavior, health, religion, and human thought, at once offering a huge number of resources to make the physical existence more meaningful and attractive –especially given its contribution concerning the continuity of life, which death does not interrupt.

Such conviction fills the dreadful existential void, encouraging individuals to pursue beauty, progress, and love in search for the state of plenitude.

In light of this knowledge, human beings are no longer the puppets of absurd and fortuitous forces that supposedly created and led them. They become the conscientious architects of their realization, developing the underlying potential that lends them beauty and waits for a chance to blossom.

Life, in its external structure, is a ceaseless *continuum* that grows increasingly attractive and challenging the more we conquer it and progress.

On account of their immortality, human beings are destined to the glory of the infinite. The *dream* of annihilation –a psychological escape mechanism from reality and the human struggle– is no more than a *nightmare* bewildering the minds of those hoping for a state of torpidity –*nothingness*– as a recourse for self-destruction, capable of eliminating the bitterness and conflict that generated existential apathy, in turn responsible for the loss of meaning, and declaring defeat in connection with aspirations about life and eternity.

Soon after publishing *The Death of God* and making the voice of a *madman* looking for God heard, Nietzsche –already the victim of personal torments– somberly took a final plunge into the abyss of insanity, passing less than a year later in an unconscious state. He somehow succeeded in depicting his own bitterness and disbelief through the character of the unhappy psychopath running toward the square looking for God.

In turn, Heine, who also consistently fought against God, affirmed on a postscript in his book *Romanzero*: "*Yes, I have returned to God. I am the prodigal son... There is a divine spark in each human being, after all.*"

On the other hand, Schopenhauer concluded: "*The physical world is not a mother, but simply the wet nurse of God's living Spirit within us.*"

The reality of Spirit survival and Spirit exchanges with humans is inbuilt in the very being. The goal of exterior phenomena is to raise awareness to this fact when humans are immersed in matter, so that their existence may be healthier, optimistic, and creative, thereby leading to continuous growth as they acquire, through new experiences, the resources that will enable them to evolve.

Such is the message that, characterizing people who pursue for the rational behavior inherent to immortality and spirit communication, is within reach of all who strive to make their existence appealing and to overcome the destructive archetypes that linger in the unconscious, which, at times, reemerge generating torment by concocting fantasies of annihilation and the destruction of life.

18
MEMORY REGRESSION

Forgetfulness of the past is a real act of God's mercy toward His children because it affords them a fresh start in a new body without the burden of tormenting memories resulting from bad deeds perpetrated in past existences. Likewise, it allows them to forget about ennobling deeds and very special affections that became references in their own progress.

Undoubtedly, the memory of unfortunate acts would cause a great deal of suffering due to remorse, which in turn would prevent the fulfillment of important responsibilities. Consequently, it could turn into dismay, generating the unfortunate desire to abandon one's duties, or fear in the face of new challenges. Besides, the detailed memory of specific incidents would also trigger the memory of the individuals involved, the victims, or those still responsible for the unfortunate event, thus increasing the animosity toward the latter.

On the other hand, if reliving glorious moments or unique relationships could be a motivation to stay in the fight, it could also encourage people to stick to specific choices to the detriment of new relationships, thereby shrinking the fraternal circle of growth in the search for the immense universal family.

We should also consider that the memories of the current existence already constitute a heavy burden to bear. If we were to add past life memories, it would undoubtedly disrupt the mechanism of homeostasis or balance, for it is not possible to handle emotions that exceed human beings' capacity for physio-psychical resistance.

The human body has a limited amount of energy to handle emotions and sensations. When this limit is exceeded, the very delicate psychical equipment is negatively impacted, suffering irreversible damage. For this reason, many interdimensional people —who simultaneously coexist in the physical and the spiritual spheres— experience hallucinations, as well as nervous and mental imbalances, difficult to heal during the physical existence if they lack morals or cannot reconcile their behavior with the psychical structure.

Despite the fact that humans remain at a stage that is more physiological than psychological —sensations over emotions— they have earned credits that have allowed them to break free from certain constrictions imposed by unfortunate acts perpetrated in past incarnations, which weigh heavily in their internal economy generating intense suffering, afflictive imbalances, problems with interpersonal relationships and sexuality, as well as economic and financial challenges that lead them to greater setbacks, when not to very distressing failures.

Given that the Divine Laws are about justice but also about love, the disregarded codes of honor must be reinstated and the lost harmony —on account of the unfortunate events— must be regained.

Atoning for our mistakes is therefore inevitable, albeit it is not absolutely necessary that such atonement involves suffering.

Jesus taught that *love covers a multitude of sins*, and when in the presence of the wayward woman who, overtaken by tenderness and repentance over the insane existence to which she had consented washed His feet at Simon's house, Jesus released her from greater suffering, comforting her with a dignifying and suggestive statement: *"Because of your great love, your sins are forgiven!"*

He certainly did not exonerate her from the consequences of her insane acts, for they would come naturally as a result of the wrong use she had made of her free will. He demonstrated that, through loving, people could be rehabilitated from any nefarious acts they may have perpetrated, provided that they commit to their rehabilitation, which is the primary goal for all those looking to grow and be happy.

Ever since the onset of mediumistic and parapsychological phenomena, researchers of the human psyche have detected that in the current archives of the psyche information about past behavior can be found, which, in a way, continues to dictate new approaches or the repetition of the offending conduct that became incised as an agent of perturbation.

In cases of ecmnesia, as well as past lives spontaneous recall, or even through hypnosis, it is possible to relive forgotten experiences whose impact can explain countless present-day occurrences.

On the other hand, backed by the infinite possibilities of the current archives of the unconscious as well as those of the deep unconscious, noble psychoanalysts have found in perinatal events the causality for many traumas, phobias, inferiority and superiority complexes, and narcissistic disorders perturbing the behavior of their patients. Through the use of the appropriate resources to that avail, successful incursions have been made thanks to which many sufferers find release from the tormenting states of their soul, as they are *cleansed* from the impressions engraved in it.

Unable to find the cause of the problems afflicting their patients in the present or even in their childhood, doctors were encouraged to lower their probe, thereby reaching deeper archives –the *collective archetypes*– which are no more than the memories of other incarnations, where the causes responsible for the disturbances were indeed found.

Having identified the causes, the effects were treated in therapy, making many enigmatic sufferings give way to an awareness regarding the causes. Said causes are then overcome by reliving the events under the guidance of a professional that helps the patient understand that these events have already taken place, so they no longer need to continue to emit devastating waves on the current psyche.

Clearly, during such evocations –whether under hypnoses or a lighter form of induction– patients do not fully remember their past incarnation. Instead, they are instructed to find the cause that triggers their particular problem.

To this challenging proposition, the unconscious responds with the harmful *matrices*, allowing for their reemergence with the patient's consequent release from their onerous burden.

Obviously, this area is still in its infancy requiring many further studies. It must be understood in greater depth to avoid new memories from increasing the load already present in the conscious mind, otherwise running the risk of upsetting the patient's homeostasis.

Besides, not all patients accessing their memories through this process will be freed from the harmful effects of their unfortunate acts. There has to be a change in their behavior for the better as well. They have to alter their mental plans identifying forgotten duties or duties that were once again neglected to be released from these karmic outcomes.

An awareness regarding humans' responsibilities in relation to life is a hugely valuable therapy to acquire physical and mental health. This is especially true about moral realization, whose often unhealthy roots can be found in the folds of the deep mind, in the foundation of the spiritual unconscious.

However, any incursion in these domains without competent and specialized guidance, devoid of noble purposes and motivated by curiosity or pointless frivolity, always ends up in disaster, that is, in an unpredictable success, frequently with a bitter taste.

Human beings are what they make of themselves. Self-knowledge and daily soul-searching –trying to identify their present and past reality– is the great challenge waiting for a fierce resolve and continuous dedication on the part of each individual.

Every bit of love and interest in self-illumination must be invested for the benefit of the evolutionary process, so that our desire for inner growth and the multiplication of our ethical, moral, and intellectual resources will not cease, producing nonstop on behalf of the good and life, in which we are irrecusably immersed.

19
HUMAN PARANORMALITY

Anthropological and psychological evolution have been shaping the human form and psyche very gently and with such calculated precision that, in comparison to their remote ancestors, contemporary humans possess great beauty, harmony, and sensibility. If fact, almost nothing reminds what humans used to look like when they took their first steps during the primitive period.

The development of science in alliance with technology, the philosophical conquests of human thought, ethical and moral progress, social adaptations, and the acquisition of artistic notions have expanded the psyche, which now blossoms in never before imagined conquests predicting boundless possibilities.

The ideal use of the senses, guided by the conscience, slowly increases peoples' capacity to journey within and search for higher and more delicate perceptions, leading them to the identification of dormant paranormal abilities. Initially, said abilities appear as scattered episodes that call their attention, inviting them to do a more careful examination regarding their unexplored potential.

Slowly but surely, these instances consolidate experiences and the cerebral being gives way to the transpersonal one; the organicist concept of life makes way for the spiritualist concept of life, and the spiritualist concept of life gives way to the Spiritist concept of life. The individual is no longer just matter, or the binary expression Spirit and matter, but instead a tridimensional being: Spirit, perispirit, and matter.

As it evolves, the *Intelligent Principle of the Universe*[11] expands a subtle and molding envelope whose deterministic purpose is felt in the physical form.

Overcoming the initial impediments created by matter, and as it in turn evolves, it assumes control of the physical impulses, which then guides in a healthy way seeking to dominate and move beyond material obstacles, to use the body without submitting to its imperious needs, to be able to move within it without constraints and to use it wisely.

Inevitably, paranormality is the next level to be conquered, as it has been happening since the beginning of the evolutionary process.

A number of remarkable Spirits who, in remote antiquity, took the plunge into the body to accelerate the moral and intellectual development of humankind and Planet Earth, possessed paraphysical abilities, which rendered evident immortality as well as the infinite possibilities inherent to all.

Given the degree psychical perception nowadays, paranormality is becoming an integral part of human

---

11. "*What is spirit?* The intelligent principle of the universe. *What is spirit's innermost nature?* It is not easy to explain spirit in your language. For you, it is nothing because it is not something palpable; nevertheless, for us it is something. You must realize that nothing means nothing, and nothing does not exist." See *The Spirits' Book*, Allan Kardec, Question 23 (International Spiritist Council, 4th Edition, Revised (2010)). – Tr.

behavior, no longer being a supernatural or miraculous phenomenon, but a *sixth sense* instead, according to the correct definition given by Prof. Charles Richet when observing the facts produced by the mediums he so carefully studied.

As a source of energy, the Spirit possesses valuable resources that express through its psyche, enabling it to radiate its thoughts to produce telepathic phenomena consciously or unconsciously; precognition and retrocognition by detecting waves specific to certain events; clairvoyance and clairaudience by detecting special frequencies associated to transpersonal events; as well as tuning into the spirit world where it originates and to which it returns.

The ability to detect waves and very delicate and complex vibratory fields favors exchanges with Spirits devoid of a physical envelope, currently living in the causal sphere of life.

Mediumship, which is a faculty of the Spirit, is *clothed in cells* in order to process communications, thus expanding the horizons of human thought and allowing individuals to dive into the infinite ocean of knowledge.

Ethical, moral, and intellectual growth has given humans a sharper perception of the extra-physical reality, allowing them to identify the inexhaustible fountains of wisdom pouring from the spirit world.

Capable of consciously using some brain functions and glands of the endocrine system, humans build antennas to detect mental waves moving within the planet's vibratory field, whether they come from incarnate beings or from Spirits that are free from the material armor.

Indeed, this phenomenon also occurs with individuals devoid of principles and sound behavior, which, nonetheless, possess the natural faculty of detection, for mediumship is in itself neutral, independent of moral credentials or any other values in the areas of religion or philosophy.

The lucid and conscientious acquisition of this ability, however, endows the person with resources for its proper use, which in turn generates inner growth and balanced behavior.

Mediumship therefore expresses through a specific energy field radiating through the perispirit, which more easily detects vibrations from other beings, since the phenomenon happens through this subtle vehicle as the instrument that registers and decodes the Spirit's mental wave directed to the medium.

The medium's moral and intellectual improvement obviously allows him or her to better filter and translate the message, helping the Spirit to communicate with greater ease. Besides, lofty feelings, good conduct, and a developed mind attract elevated Spirits wishing to contribute to the progress of the medium in particular, and society in general.

Freed from taboos and ceremonial rites once associated with it, mediumship begins to acquire citizenship for the remarkable contributions it makes to human knowledge and culture, science and reason, awakening minds to the important responsibilities concerning the physical existence as well as beings' physical, emotional, and psychical health.

Intrinsic to the human soul, when mediumship exteriorizes in an ostensive way, it requires discipline and education, so that its irruption and natural course may cause no harm to the medium.

As a delicate instrument for communication, mediumship requires that mediums lead healthy lives to avoid physical and mental exhaustion. Conversely, it should generate well-being and joy due to the inspirations and vibratory resilience it brings.

Mediumistic resources increase with practice, bringing forth a whole host of elevated thoughts and ideas that encourage service, social progress, and individual as well as collective harmony.

When ignored, mediumship causes various problems. Since psychical attunement with the spirit world happens spontaneously –and generally within the same frequency as the medium's– he or she attracts similar beings or those at a lower level which establish a connection through *vibratory osmosis*, taking up energy that is essential for the physical body.

This phenomenon, which is very common –much more than people think–happens frequently and answers for many apparent illnesses appearing biological but having a mediumistic origin instead, on their way to becoming episodes of spirit obsession –physical, mental, or both simultaneously– that turn into severe diseases of the soul.

Firmly guided through the study of its physiology and the moral requirements it imposes, meditation, inner silence and the practice of the good and service, it amplifies its capacity for detection to such an extent that the transit between the two spheres –the physical and the spiritual– becomes easy, serene, and comfortable.

Likewise, the development of animic[12] abilities –those that originate in our own Spirit– make us more sensitive regarding the existential reality; enrich us with beauty; enable us to exchange thoughts and actions with other individuals thereby breaking the chains that have kept us at a distance; and help us to contribute more decidedly in favor of a new

---

12. Animic: In Spiritism, it refers to psychic phenomena produced by the incarnate Spirit without the intervention of other Spirits (e.g. telepathy, telekinesis, psychometry, among others). –Tr.

social order –more just and equitable– which will make life on earth better and more enriching.

As paranormality develops in these two aspects, human beings will increasingly incorporate extra physical resources. In the future they will use said ability consciously and securely just as they use the conventional senses today –which were acquired over long periods of time in multifarious incarnations.

20
SPIRITUAL PARASITISM

Having taken the dimension of a real epidemic currently —just as it was the case at other times throughout humankind's history— spiritual parasitism, or spirit obsession, is a terrible scourge that afflicts human beings, overburdening them with diseases difficult to diagnose and even more difficult to treat.

In every case of spirit obsession there is always an alarming instance of conflicting feelings between the adversaries, who go after one another with a great deal of cruelty as they pursue their despicable agenda.

A remnant of the animal ancestry that endures in the Spirit, when individuals feel wronged or betrayed, disrespected or hurt in their financial interests they attack those they consider their adversaries, inflicting torments that can end up as real tragedies.

Incapable of understanding the illness or the ignorance predominating in those responsible for their unhappiness, they become killers of the soul, feeding their hate and planning their revenge with which they believe to be doing *justice by their own hands,* as if the universal Sovereign Laws needed their services to reestablish the balance upset by recklessness everywhere.

Blinded by the madness that has possessed them and eager to retaliate, they do not hesitate to create tormenting and deeply distressing situations, thus initiating a process of psychical connection that evolves into a controlling hypnosis and culminates as a cruel, vampire-like parasitism.

This all-out war is about unresolved offenses committed by the current victim who, at present, lacks reliable information to not fall into the trap expertly set by the enemy from beyond the grave.

The process can begin as a nervous imbalance; visual or auditory hallucinations; feelings of ill at ease and restlessness; anxiety or frustration; insecurity or intense suspicion; as well as rebellion or excessive mental fixation, but it can also irrupt suddenly, as a violent episode that disconnects the psychical components in the form of insanity.

The process is more excruciating when it begins subtly and gains traction gradually, until the usurper's mind ultimately takes control by causing bewilderment and disturbances, telepathically inducing the person to leave the physical existence by self-neglect, mistreating everyone around them, or by suicide.

The avenging Spirit fails to realize that, with this attitude, it behaves in the same way as the person responsible for its unhappiness, thereby sowing the seeds for *tomorrow's* negative consequences.

Even if we have had our feelings hurt by disloyalty or infamy, we do not have the right to seek revenge turning into merciless creditors.

The Sovereign Codes of Justice have the appropriate mechanisms to settle conflicts or transgressions of the Laws, without generating new debtors. Jesus was very clear when He said, *"Scandal is necessary, but woe to the person through whom scandal happens"*!

No one has the right to become a ruthless restorer of the Laws of harmony using his or her own inefficient means.

Therefore, when any kind of disharmony arises on account of someone's dysfunction, the responsible party disrupts the order, whose consequences start to revolve around it until order is once again restored.

Spirit obsession is, therefore, a state of moral misery of a Spirit that assumes the role of avenger.

Insidious and persistent, the obsessive idea penetrates the target's mind becoming an unbearable presence in both the mental and emotional realms.

It begins with a vague impression that slowly gains ground until it dominates as a persistent idea that puts down roots, creating a network of imbalance and insanity.

Long-standing spirit obsessions affect the body, shaping up into obstinate and devastating illnesses.

The phenomenon of spirit obsession can only take place when there is perfect attunement between the agent causing the perturbation and the patient, due to the *guilty conscience* that exists in the individual responsible for the problem.

Persevering in its unhealthy attempt, the aggressor insists by undermining the target's energy reserves until it is defeated. At that point, spiritual parasitism is established.

Due to the psychical exchange becoming reciprocal, as time goes by the invader of the mental domain falls victim to its own plot, becoming dependent of its vampire-like action.

At this point, a *need for nourishing* sets in, further complicating the problematic condition and requiring careful therapy for both patients...

Spirit obsession is a cruel process to restore the balance in those who do not allow themselves to progress through the excellent opportunities that love provides, getting caught in the constrictive nets of hatred, resentment, the need for revenge, and lower passions...

In order to attenuate and triumph over this scourge, there is an indispensable need for prayer, patience, a renewal of the patient's moral goals, a commitment to the practice of liberating deeds, and –almost always– a support group that should begin at home, since the relatives living with the patient are involved in the same purifying mechanism.

When the *spiritual parasite* –which enjoys the persecution– realizes is being combated, it either grows more violent or changes the strategy to dishearten the incarnate patient in order to proceed with its cherished plans for revenge.

Spirit obsession –which manifests as mental mechanisms such as telepathy, vexatious inspirations, the desire for numbing pleasure, and vile sentiments– usually extends to the physical body as it gains inner resonance on the part of the person under siege, creating the conditions for the onset of physical illnesses or functional problems that turn into severe disturbances.

Still, the therapeutic process has to obey the same rules, choosing reading material that promotes personal harmony and engaging in healthy conversations –even if it is hard– so that their current associations may give way to the higher help that is generally received.

It is true that in the most severe cases, such as fascination[13] and subjugation[14], patients have a harder time committing to their wholesome goals or even think about them. However, a genuine desire to break free from their oppression qualifies them to receive more help from both sides of life, thereby lessening the malicious interference.

Every bit of mental space dedicated to the cultivation of positive and healthy thoughts is a victory over the invader, which had previously appropriated the space to instill fear, unease, and submission.

All relentless thoughts that try to prevail in the mind signal the beginning of a negative spiritual interference laying the groundwork for spirit obsession.

Despite the fact that spirit obsession manifests in very broad and varied ways, the most common type —and which affects humans more often than not— originates in the spirit world and demands immediate action.

At present, it has reached epidemic proportions, just as it occurred at other times during the history of humankind,

---

13. Fascination: It refers to a delusion created directly by a Spirit in the thoughts of a medium, which in a certain manner paralyzes his or her capacity to judge the quality of the communications. Fascinated mediums do not believe themselves to be deceived. These Spirits manage to inspire them with a blind confidence that prevents them from realizing the deception and comprehending the absurdity of what they write, even when it jumps out at the eyes of everyone else. The delusion can reach the point to where it causes them to consider the most ridiculous language as something sublime. Allan Kardec, *The Mediums' Book*, Ch. XXIII, #239 (International Spiritist Council (2007)) – Tr.

14. Subjugation: A constriction that causes its victims' will to become paralyzed, making them act in spite of themselves. In other words, they find themselves under true *bondage*. Allan Kardec, Part Two, Ch. XXIII #240 of *The Mediums' Book* (International Spiritist Council (2007)). – Tr.

becoming unbearable due to the moral backwardness of individuals and the predominance of their primitive passions that drove them into bloody wars, extreme moral abuses, and savage and barbaric situations…

In such instances, the earthly population and that of low-level spirits unify in an uncanny alliance where psychical symbioses become physical and vice versa.

The day before Calvary marks one of those terrible historic moments, in which the masses, flogged by the *forces of evil,* chose Barabbas over Jesus and led The Just One to His crucifixion in a spectacle that was as ludicrous as it was dishonorable.

The victimized Master knew about the indignant plot, and for this reason, He always confronted obsessor spirits as well as obsessed individuals in His capacity as Therapist par excellence. He never neglected to redirect obsessor spirits to the spiritual spheres, teaching their victims how to break free from the unfortunate bondage and how to avert similar situations in the future.

His authority sent bad Spirits away who, nonetheless, challenged Him, trying to confront Him with cynicism and irony.

Human beings are the sum total of their immediate and remote past experiences, through which they build their own future.

Therefore, the past is always present in individuals, and the future is being constantly built with the things they consent to do.

So, Spirit obsessions that result from negative actions still attached to a person's evolutionary economy will disappear once the person changes for the better, allowing for the advent of the kingdom of equanimity, justice, and love on the Earth.

21
BRIEF ESSAY ON REINCARNATION

From time immemorial, as far as humans are able to remember, evidence about the immortality of the soul, its communicability, and reincarnation is present in almost all peoples, cultures, ethnicities, and social groups, constituting one of the oldest demonstrations about the reality of beings, which are not purely circumscribed to a clump of cells and cartilage in their molecular conformation.

Walking alongside human progress and emerging at the precise moment when human thought appeared, this knowledge has advanced across millennia, inciting reflection and guiding people in the direction of higher goals that would free them from their primitive condition.

Step-by-step, the spirit climbs toward its glorious destination.

This saga –the knowledge of the eternal values– is the result of the inspiration that the immortals always gave to their peers on the Earth.

Through spirit communication we were taught about life before and after the phenomena of birth and death, giving rise to the evolutionary mechanism in a constant come-and-go, thanks to which coarse matter can release an angel by way of reincarnation.

In the most primitive cultures, reincarnation shines in the concept of metempsychosis, even if in an aggressive way characteristic of their developmental stage, demonstrating the inexorability of the *Law of Justice*, which rewards and disciplines each individual according to his or her attitude in relation to self and the Sovereign Codes of Life.

In countless barbarian tribes, the concept of metempsychosis appeared as the inevitable way to achieve growth, releasing people from their aggression and primitivism while acquiring meekness and harmony.

Beings take great pains to ascend, smoothing the rough edges and improving their feelings while in contact with experiences that instill values meant to become a process of sublimation in the direction of their immortality.

Created by God and inevitably programmed to arrive at what is right, good, beautiful, and perfect, the entire human journey must be accomplished by means of spontaneous choice and the free will humans enjoy. This makes for an impartial mechanism of justice that avoids the preferential treatment characteristic of orthodox and prejudiced doctrines.

Reincarnation is the real solution to every problem emerging in individual and collective behavior, establishing processes of human ennoblement within everyone's reach.

This remarkable philosophical concept –which can be proven in the lab– is in itself the most efficient method for Spirits to ascend. Spirits do not stagnate forever, nor do they regress, for what they have acquired in one phase is automatically transferred to the next, stockpiling said acquisitions in their extrasensory or perispiritual memory.

Prof. Francis Bowen, an eminent philosopher at Harvard University, very appropriately stated that approximately ninety-eight percent of the atoms in the human body are substituted by others due to the air, nourishment, and hydration indispensable for its upkeep during a period of one year. However, this percentage increases to one hundred percent after fifty-three weeks. So, a seventy-five-year-old person has already gone through seventy new bodies –brains included. Even if we consider that brain neurons are not included in this process, it would be very hard to conceive the possibility of the continuity of an unaltered personality –individuality– as well as character, intelligence, and emotion.

In turn, American philosopher and psychologist William James –the father of Pragmatism– elucidated that "*one may instead conceive the mental world behind the veil in as individualistic form as one pleases, without any detriment to the general scheme by which the brain is represented as a transmissive organ...*"

Evidently, the eminent student of human behavior and human thought breaks free from the brain to propose a mind-based reality, which transfers from one physical form to another as it promotes growth, gathering more significant amounts of information that exceed what is possible in a single physical existence.

The rudimentary concept of metempsychosis –though appropriate for primal cultures– gradually gave way to the concept of reincarnation, which allows for an evolutionary mechanism without retrogression, enabling Spirits to broaden their mental and moral horizons in an uninterrupted spiritual ascension.

In order for primitive humans to conceive the Divinity –considering the stage of their thought– they had to resort to the anthropomorphic model, where the Divinity is represented by parameters existing in their intellect, their fears and needs, thereby formulating punitive and rewarding concepts.

Their behavior would determine in which living expression of Nature they would return.

In a certain way, the principle for this evolutionary reality was inbuilt, according to which the psyche *sleeps* in the mineral, *dreams* in the plant, *feels* in the animal, and *thinks* in the human, when physical factors allow them to acquire intelligence –which is innate– and feelings –which are in a latent state– leading them to the point of sublimation.

The belief regarding reincarnation is so ingrained in the history of human thought that some archeologists think that during the New Stone Age, approximately 10,000–5000 BCE, corpses were buried in a fetal position to facilitate the rebirth of those who inhabited them.

This belief was based on the supposition that peoples with such funeral rites had devised them to allow for rebirth in future lives.

As a consequence of this belief, we also nowadays think that the cleaning and preparation rites done on corpses are somehow an indication of the acceptance that the Spirit will be reborn.

Many tribes –still in the primitive evolutionary phase– believed that rebirth greatly depended on how the previous body was buried, which resulted in the practice of special cares that have now evolved into what we know as preservation and beautification methods before cremation or even burial.

With regards to the Egyptian approach, however, there are differing opinions. According to some experts, the purpose of mummification was to preserve the form in order to avoid an immediate reincarnation. Others contend that it helped the reincarnated being find food, objects, and past belongings in order to continue to fulfill their commitments.

Moving past the mythological phase per se, characteristic of these primitive peoples, reincarnation reemerges in very well defined philosophical and religious content within Zoroastrianism, a doctrine derived from Zoroaster's thoughts, which was a name given to various teachers, the last of whom lived seven-hundred years BCE. He taught that human souls are immortal Spirits that descended from on High to undergo countless earthly existences, in a long succession of physical bodies, in order to acquire knowledge and experience to then happily return to the bosom of the Divinity that created them.

Later, Herodotus, Plato, and Plutarch asserted that reincarnation was the widespread belief in Egypt, albeit there was also the concept of metempsychosis: a serious and drastic method utilized to scare the esoterics, generally considered incapable of penetrating the secret meaning of spiritual revelation.

We can already see that there is clear information regarding forgetfulness of the past –the previous existence– upon the process of rebirth, as a mechanism to prevent unnecessary affliction in order to facilitate the Spirit's ascent.

The *Hermetica* is a repository of information about earthly rebirths seen as fundamental for self-illumination, given a Spirit's impossibility to reach high levels of transcendence and acquire profound knowledge in only one earthly existence.

Hinduism, in turn, as the oldest organized religion known to date, adopted reincarnation as the basis for the improvement of spiritual beings, without which said improvement would be impossible.

Buddhism, following the same ancestral behavioral lines as Hindu thought, is essentially based on reincarnation, which allows for the unfolding of the deep self's innate potential, providing liberation from the world of illusion as well as the perfect integration with the state of plenitude to which beings are destined since the moment they were created.

Past life memories have no meaning whatsoever in that doctrine, given the Spirit's upcoming awakening after the death of its body.

Since meeting Brahma is the Spirit's goal and, therefore, its main motivation for rebirth, knowing what happened in the past is of secondary importance.

Karma, in turn, is the universal causality, according to which every cause has an inevitable effect that requires atonement when the action is negative, or generates encouragement and progress when based on moral, artistic, or intellectual accomplishments; in other words, anything that promotes the individual and society.

Since the 4th century BCE, Taoism, which is a path, complementing Confucianism and Chinese Buddhism, affirms that *The Tao has always existed, even before heaven and earth, and it will continue to exist, formless, solitary, unchanging, reaching everywhere without sustaining any kind of harm, eternal, as the mother of the Universe. All else is a continuous flow.*

Approximately three hundred years ago, the eminent Chuang Tzu —one of its first philosophers— stated that *"Having reached the human form must always be a reason for joy, to then go through innumerable transitions with only the infinite before us... what a superlative blessing!"*

Some Islamic schools of thought admit reincarnation and propose it as an uplifting method to reach Heaven. They affirm the return of Muhammad al Muntazar (Muhammad), who *disappeared* in the year 878, but continues to live, and is expected to return to save the world.

In a certain way it is similar to Jesus' *promised Consoler* alive in Spiritism.

Sikhism, a more recent doctrine that came to light with Nanak, born in 1466 – Nanak himself affirms to having been reborn innumerable times and having performed many good and bad deeds– proposes the wheel of *samsara,* from which Spirits must break free to grow and unfold their latent divine potential through the practice of good deeds, respect for God's Laws, and prayer –all efficient ways to achieve said freedom.

In Greece, Pherecydes was the first thinker to refer to reincarnation in his *Theologia,* known as *Seven Adyta.* He was the teacher of Pythagoras who taught this same belief in his *School of Croton.*

Pythagoras himself believed to have been Euphorbus, wounded by Menelaus in Troy; Hermotimus, who recognized Euphorbus' shield while at a Temple of Apollo, and later Pyrrhus, a fisherman from Delos.

Pindar, and mainly Plato, not only believed in reincarnation but also worked on its dissemination. Plato, in particular, inspired by his master Socrates, immortalized his belief in his major works *Republic, Phaedo, Meno, Timaeus,* and *Laws,* where he teaches about the immortality of the soul and shares his transit through an unlimited number of rebirths to finally return to the world of ideas after having conquered beauty, truth, and goodness, which are acquired in the course of evolutionary experiences.

According to Plato, the choice of old friends, relatives, and dear ones result from one's awareness, wisdom, and moral achievements.

In Rome, reincarnation was highly respected by many philosophers such as Posidonius and Virgil. Virgil affirmed that souls, after wandering around the abyss, drink water from the Lethe –the river of forgetfulness– before returning to the body. Sallust for example, taught that our current congenital afflictions are the natural consequence of past experiences.

Later, Philo, a Jew from Alexandria, confirmed reincarnation explaining that God created all souls pure but, after making their choice between good and evil –free will– the reincarnation cycle began.

With the advent of Christianity, reincarnation found a very solid foundation in the teachings of Christ, particularly during His encounter with Nicodemus; in the revelation regarding Elijah's return as John the Baptist; when He referred to settling debts and its consequences; the case of the man who was *blind from* birth, and many other extraordinary examples.

Jesus' promises are based on divine Justice, in which we find *reincarnation*, allowing us to rehabilitate from our mistakes –through self-forgiveness– and to advance –through the practice of noble actions– demonstrating God's love for all of God's children.

Jesus never criticized physical rebirths in His teachings, by which Spirits have an opportunity to grow and achieve self-illumination.

Continuing with the favorable testimonies in regard to reincarnation, Neo-Platonism –founded by Ammonius Saccas in 193 BCE. – produced a significant number of thinkers and *Church Fathers* who theologically demonstrated its factuality.

We could mention Origen as one such example. He affirmed that souls could live without bodies, for bodies are of secondary importance considering that spiritual life is the real life.

In turn, Plotinus –another disciple of Ammonius Saccas– asserted that reincarnation is a purifying process for those who make mistakes. However, influenced by metempsychosis, he also taught that bad persons return in *inferior forms* such as that of plants and animals, which is not what really happens in the process of evolution. Perhaps, that esoteric concept may have been intended to cause the exoterics to fear justice, given their lack of psychological maturity to understand love's sovereign guidelines.

Porphyry, who was aware of the multiplicity of physical existences clearly stated, *"A being that has experienced different lives (existences) –some better and some worse– becomes a more competent judge than a being that knew but one . . . "* And he went on to say, *"Someone who lives guided by the intellect . . . has passed through the irrational life..."* Furthermore, he said, *"After their pilgrimage, the souls of the philosophers are forever set free because they were purified by reincarnation."*

Iamblichus, in turn, explained that apparent injustices derive from past life behavior, since the *gods* see everything and make all the right provisions for the irrepressible process of evolution in which beings are immersed.

St. Gregory Nazianzen confirmed the progression of Spirits through reincarnation, and so did St. Jerome in his *Letter to Avitus*. St. Jerome further stated that reincarnation was practiced and accepted by primitive Christians.

Macrobius presented the soul as a pure being –at the time of its creation– that descends to experience the contingency of matter but returns to its realm of origin purified of all imperfections once again.

Demonstrating this process of spiritual growth, Proclus affirmed that a Spirit could be reborn in the form of a beast, but never as a beast.[15]

Celts and Gauls furthered the belief in reincarnation through the Druid teachings and it continued with the Gnostics, such as the Cathars or Albigensians.

Ever since the Council of Constantinople, reincarnation became a heretic doctrine thanks to the petulance of Emperor Justinian. The assembly gathered by him opened the door to persecutions that would later take place through the Inquisition and every mechanism of medieval intolerance, which extended into the Modern Age.

However, there are no promulgated condemnations against the doctrine of reincarnation in the Catholic Church, whether from councils, encyclicals, or other official documents of the faith. They are rather scattered, periodic opinions.

Though reincarnation was always criticized by some *fathers of the Church* as well as various philosophers and skeptics, it has remained alive throughout the centuries reappearing in the most diverse cultures.

The belief in reincarnation reemerged even in the Middle Ages, and without completely disappearing during the period of the persecutions, in *Dante's* thoughts and poetry, when, in

---

15. *"Could a spirit that has animated a human body incarnate in an animal?"* "That would be a regression, and a spirit does not regress. The river does not flow back to its source. (See question 118)." Question 612, *The Spirits' Book*, Allan Kardec (International Spiritist Council, 4th Edition, Revised (2010)).

(Question 118: *"Can spirits regress?"* "No. As they progress, they gain an understanding of what is holding them back from perfection. When a spirit finishes a particular trial, it never forgets the knowledge it acquired. A spirit may remain stationary, but it never regresses.") – Tr.

Paradise, the bard affirmed: *He returned from Hell to his bones . . . the glorious soul returns to the flesh where it lived for some time.*

The Medici family –thanks to Marcilio Ficino's translations, which updated the thought of Plotinus, Iamblichus, Synesius and others, thus enabling its dissemination– lent great credibility to reincarnation.

Giordano Bruno defended it and later accepted it.

Erasmus, cardinal Nicholas of Cusa, and great thinkers such as the Count of St. Germain –from the court of Louis XIV– Van Helmont, Leibnitz, and Voltaire –who said that *it was not more surprising to be born twice than once,* were defenders of reincarnation.

In Nature, everything is resurrection.

Napoleon claimed to be the reincarnation of Charlemagne. Immanuel Kant shared his belief in the process through which souls went on to inhabit other planets after having concluded their cycle of lives on the Earth.

There are hundreds of writers, poets, thinkers, and scientists that have explicitly avowed their belief in reincarnation due to the justice of the evolutionary process. Among them –and just to name a few– Honoré de Balzac, Emerson, Longfellow, Edgar Allan Poe, Tennyson, Thoreau, Walt Whitman, Bulwer Lytton, George Elliot, James Joyce, Walter Scott, Thomas Carlyle, Lowes Dickinson, Jack London, Søren Kierkegaard, Tolstoy, Gustav Mahler, Robert Browning, Rudyard Kipling, Thomas Moore, Thomas Edison, Victor Hugo, Gustave Flaubert, Eduard Schuré, Oscar Wilde, Francis Thompson, Yeats…

Without reincarnation, how could we understand the differences in destinies, behaviors, tendencies, and inclinations, if all souls were created at the same time and were destined to choose their future by behaving in a way that is not in line with their own possibilities? What resources would be available to someone suffering from insanity, schizophrenia, severe congenital malformations, or whose capacity for discernment is impaired due to severe limitations or dysfunction? Besides, how can we conceive that the *blood of the Just One* rescued everyone who could not be baptized or were unable to join this or that religious denomination in which the elements for salvation were found?

The terrible manifestations of people's destinies – with their shocking differences– cannot originate in the Divine Will setting out to test the fragile human incapable of choosing what to do and how to do it. Furthermore, let us consider that when a finite being makes a mistake it cannot deserve an eternal punishment –as is the case of those thrown in hell without remission. Likewise, in eternal punishments we see the failure of God's infinite Love, since it could not save a being created *in God's image* from the being's inherent fragility. This would imply that perfection also created imperfection, love generated the absence of love, and goodness produced evil...

God *aspires* for humanity to reach the perfection to which it has been destined, but it must be the consequence of personal effort, for striving and struggling confer dignity to the Spirit.

Precocious genius, a higher sense of aesthetics, and altruistic feelings cannot share the same source with criminal tendencies and a penchant for destruction...

Created simple –albeit endowed with a vast potential– the Spirit advances through personal effort and gradually grows until it reaches stellar glory thanks to reincarnation.

When we observe behavioral conflict and questionable morals; anguish and perturbing complexes; emotional torments and anxiety; dilacerating, degenerative, and irreversible illnesses; intense hatred and love; unwarranted mistrust, arrogance, pride, and extreme selfishness; backwardness and wisdom; gentleness and brutality; noble attitudes and baseness; and saintly gestures and barbarity coexisting side-by-side, how can we conceive that those individuals had but one opportunity?

Reincarnation is the key to explain not just such instances, but all instances differentiating individuals, even as we search for the genetic explanation for most physical, mental, and behavioral phenomena, given that the very genetic explanation is the consequence of a choice made by the Spirit to mold –through its perispirit– the physical envelope it needs to settle debts, to make amends, and grow.

Beings are responsible for their own destiny, elaborating the physical body indispensable for their process of self-illumination –which everyone must go through.

There is ample documentation to this avail in childhood spontaneous memories; dreams about past lives; painful and destructive episodes of spirit obsession; revelations received through mediumistic communication; and *déjà-vu*, in its various modalities such as *déjà-entendu, déjà-éprouvè, déjà-senti,* and déjà-raconté, which can originate in the vague memory of something that has already happened, or has already been understood, felt, heard, and lived; in the lucid memories regarding events that were actually experienced… And beyond them, there is knowledge of the past through meditation –when helpful to the person's evolution– or even rising from spiritual persecutions whose matrices are found in unfortunate behaviors of the past.

Both deep trance hypnosis and superficial hypnosis have made remarkable contributions for the corroboration of past lives.

Reincarnation announcements are a real challenge to any kind of doubt, particularly due to the details furnished before the formation of the fetus that are later corroborated.

Likewise, present-day markings attesting to the way in which the Spirit died in its last incarnation are a strong proof for the thesis of reincarnation.

There are certainly various hypotheses against reincarnation, which get lost in an intricate tangle of theories that do not hold up to tests done in the lab. Albeit respectable possibilities no doubt, they are more improbable than then one they try to negate or destroy.

More exuberant that the personality is the individuality –the very being– which appears at each rebirth with its own characteristics, shaped by past actions that preexist and survive the physical body.

In reality, a person's behavior is what programs the future, which becomes an individual, familial or collective karmic phenomenon for cities and nations, a process of purification or a reason for happiness for those who incurred it.

In this context, forgetfulness of the past is a blessing that cannot be overlooked because –exception made with being released from certain afflictions or reaching higher goals– forgetfulness of the past helps individuals select values and objectives, for everyone is, nonetheless, led in a certain way by unconscious reminiscences resurfacing as tendencies, aptitudes, idiosyncrasies, interests, or indifference at the time of choosing behavior, professions, or goals.

If we had access to past life memories –particularly unhappy ones such as tragedies, harmed suffered, crimes, anguish, and reversals of fortune– our psychophysical homeostasis would be upset and, therefore, it would not be possible for us to continue with our process of evolution. Rebirth would be unsuitable, if not harmful.

Similarly, memories of joy, happiness, blissful and loving moments, and enchanting chapters would generate an intense nostalgia, when not profound despair over the loss of such gratifying times as opposed to the afflictive experiences we must currently face.

Arguments attempting to show past life memory as something positive at the time of choosing better partners and behavior are incorrect, given the selfishness that prevails in human nature. Besides, past life memory would also trigger the recall of everyone who has been a part of our lives along with their weaknesses, mistakes, and offenses committed.

The subconscious mind releases reminiscences –both good and bad– that are useful to a person's ascent, helping, without imposing, in the construction of better days ahead.

Everyone must have good and bad experiences in order to imprint in the innermost recesses of their being that which edifies and that which perturbs, choosing what will always serve as a guide.

Ignorance and unawareness respond for human suffering as they generate the pain that bolts them to the ground of primitivism. As humans gain more understanding, they elevate themselves and unfold their entire loving potential, which is waiting for the right moment to reveal itself.

Lucid awareness is the road to spiritual ascension – mainly when the forces of love craft the wings of angelhood.

For this reason, during the interval between incarnations –depending on the being's evolutionary level– the Spirit experiences other states in preparation for its physical rebirth. It programs future experiences, accompanies the process of cultural, moral, and spiritual development characteristic of these other states, which incidentally must be transferred to the physical realm to promote the world and its inhabitants.

It can be a long or a short period, according to the needs of each individual. It is an opportunity for mental recovery and cleansing in preparation for the next journey in the flesh.

The knowledge about reincarnation implies responsibility instead of complacency and dynamic behavior instead of stagnation, since the person knows that his or her evolutionary process will be the product of personal choice.

When this does not happen –the choice of values in line with the good– suffering sets in, followed by the urgent need for self-transformation, a painful process that can and should be avoided.

Said mechanism –reincarnation– enables the conquest of love, for it was elaborated by God –Absolute Love– to attract God's children toward the state of plenitude for which they have been destined.

The process of reincarnation begins when the sperm fertilizes the egg and continues until the beginning of adolescence, when the complementary sexual characteristics are set.

Therefore, the awareness of the fact that we are building the future is the right kind of stimulus to remain engaged in any kind of struggle, generating peace and the joy of living.

Thus, when dealing with any eventuality, we must carefully ponder the consequences, by which we will forge the heavy chains that bind us to painful recapitulations or we will sublimate the form, transforming it into an essence that will rise in the direction of freedom.

22
THE PLURALITY OF
INHABITED WORLDS

Given the reiterated human interest to find proof about the possibility of life on other planets —particularly through the most recent studies conducted by the rover *Sojourner* launched by the rocket *Pathfinder* in the direction of Mars, to confirm suspicions, through careful studies and molecular comparisons with rocks found on Mars, that the meteorites fallen on Antarctica came indeed from that planet–– there is a challenging task ahead.

Excited about these rock fragments referred to as SNC, astronomers expected that the analysis done on *the red planet* would determine that the fissures in the rocks –if they in indeed came from Mars– would contain evidence of microscopic organisms, which would point to the presence of some form of life from a past slightly over 30 billion years...

The results of the studies of the Martian rocks, however, were somewhat disappointing, demonstrating that they were similar to those on the earth and, therefore, different from the meteorite fragments under observation.

Life, which always seems to repeat itself, on the Earth has characteristics appropriate to its constitution expressed in the human form –as we know it– as well as in other forms resulting from mesological factors conducive to their manifestation. As the environment changes, life then undoubtedly presents itself in keeping with the different parameters characteristic to the evolutionary adaptations and needs.

Besides, considering that life is not just a cellular conglomerate, but is also present in the field of energy where the *intelligent principle* dwells –therefore, not requiring matter to exist– matter is only an opportune accessory for the development of latent potential.

Observing the universe, however, approximately over 100 billion galaxies are detected being that the galaxy where the earth is located has 250 billion stars and looks like a cloud of *sidereal dust* spreading across immeasurable space.

According to Astronomy experts, our galaxy would have the shape of a tetra-dimensional hyperboloid, deserving from Albert Einstein a description as a tetra-dimensional hyper-cylinder, measuring 120,000 light–years in length with a 30,000 light–years' diameter.

In this colossal proposition, the Solar System has almost no significance; it could be considered *a lost speck of dust* with no astronomical relevance.

Considering the *Big Bang* as being the origin of the Cosmos 15 billion years ago –something that, by the way, is highly arguable given that stars have been detected whose origin would date back to well before that time– but starting from the materialistic premise that all celestial bodies were created at the time of the Big Bang, those that were dislocated from the epicenter and managed to condense sooner than the earth would have specific conditions for the manifestation of life, which would now be at a more advanced stage compared to present-day humankind.

Therefore, in our galaxy if we considered the possibility that around each star there are a number of planets in gravitational orbit, it would be obvious to suppose that there would be millions of planets where life would unfold according to the conditions known to us, since they originated in the central hub where our world originated.

Our small earth, however, strikes us as being gigantic because it has a mass of 6 sextillion tons, which equals to a specific mass of 5,5 grams per cubic centimeter. However, the Sun –which sustains life on earth– is 1,300.000 times larger, and has a mass that is 333,432 times more voluminous than that of the earth.

In turn, the Sun is many times smaller than first-magnitude stars like Canopus, Sirius, Betelgeuse, and Antares, which triumphantly sing a hymn of praise to the Creation.

Advancing their studies into the unfathomable sidereal abysses, astrophysicists have detected blue quasars, which are almost inexhaustible sources of radio waves, with an average distance of 5 to 10 light-years between them. The amount of radio waves emitted by each one of them per second equals to what would be given off by the disintegration of 1 billion suns.

Careful investigation shows that the universe continues to expand, and while some particles are flying away from the epicenter where they originated, others are flying back.

Rapidly advancing their knowledge of the Cosmos, they have discovered that it results in its entirety from a peculiar black substance still to be photographed because of its invisibility, yet responsible for almost everything that exists in it. On account of its peculiarity, said substance would be made up of neutrinos –a fundamental particle conceived by German physicist, Wolfgang Pauli, in 1930 and only detected by high-speed photography deep underground in 1955– which despite being considered to be matter has no mass and no magnetic or electrical fields. Nonetheless it is present in the entire universe.

The most audacious observations made thanks to the images provided and transmitted by the Hubble telescope in orbit around the earth, have detected the continued birth of new galaxies as well as the death of stars and other conglomerates, which are absorbed by the gravitational force of what came to be known as *black holes*.

And one wonders, what would be the purpose of an unknown, infinite, and ever-unfolding Universe, whose grandeur hasn't even been entirely fathomed, if there was no life outside the earth?

After this question, others would follow. For example, is there only one Universe, or could there be others beyond the relative infinite? And, what existed before the Universe?

The materialistic paradigm dreams about the presence of forces that annihilated one another ceaselessly in that *nothingness* that existed before the universe, until the time when *something* altered one of the fields causing the big explosion that signals the beginning of it all.

And human imagination gets lost in tormenting searches to deny the intelligent universal Causality that generated the known effects, and others which have not yet been detected, exclusively fueled by a pathological desire to reduce everything to a chaotic occurrence.

Despite this stubborn and ongoing negativistic obstinacy, logic derived from reason hovers above all doubts, affirming that life is not the legacy of chance, the void, or nothingness.

As an inevitable consequence, life manifests in various and unimaginable dimensions, filling the entire world with energy –wherever it may be– and endowed with intelligence where conditions allow for it to grow and evolve.

Jesus, the Builder of the Earth, looking at the vastness of the celestial bodies, wisely and with thorough knowledge on the matter said, back in the day, *"In my father's house, there are many mansions..."* And Allan Kardec, the loyal disciple, based on Spirit communication and his characteristic ironclad logic confirmed the plurality of inhabited worlds, which are spiritual homes, where beings pass through on their way to perfection.

The day space travel eventually allows humans to personally visit Mars –after having landed on the Moon, where they will erect platforms that allow for such daring jumps– they will gain more ample knowledge about the reality of life and the immortal Spirits that we are, thereby becoming better prepared to bow before the greatness of the Creator with profound reverence, and to sing a hymn of praise to life, in which they are immersed and from which they cannot escape.

23
MYTH AND FANTASY

An archetypical inheritance from our journey through the early stages of the evolution of human thought, human beings remain subject to the influence of myths, which change in appearance but continue to subjugate and impose themselves as a path for cultural development or as escapes from reality through trends that appear periodically.

Mythological figures of the Graeco-Roman Pantheon or the almighty gods of the Eastern cultural legacy have made a comeback with remarkable force in the different periods of old civilizations. In present-day society, they have become a dominant force.

The resurgence of barbarian cultures adopted by modern youth pursuing exhibitionistic goals not only resuscitates atavisms left over from previous incarnations –still alive in the unconscious– but also violent expressions of the survival instinct –aggressive in nature out of the need for defense mechanisms and self-realization– attracting attention to hide inner conflict, shyness, and a fear of society. This leads to the creation of groups in which members can identify, hide, and give free reign to their primitivism.

On the other hand, myths that remain alive in individuals generate new *gods* to which they submit creating their own language to communicate among themselves –something that makes them feel as one of the elected– depredating and acting aggressively toward other social groups, and self-consuming due to the use of illicit drugs in terrible altered states of consciousness that manifest as loss of balance and death.

The exaggerated *cult of the body* evokes the subjacent Hellenic period and the gladiators' ideal, as they earned glory by killing and promoting the destructive *ego* in detriment of the deep and fulfilling *Self.*

When, in the past, this was not possible, the myths of the triumphant heroes were expressed in wars through endless, destructive battles where astuteness, wickedness and crime always predominated, ousting reason and the conscience so that ravaging barbarism would prevail.

In contrast, positive ancestral myths became instruments to encourage growth for countless generations fascinated by these archetypes inherent to humans, and which derive from the living forces of Nature.

Due to anthropological, sociological, and psychological development, identification of the myth as an evolutionary resource has undergone a necessary rereading, concluding that myths, more often than not, transforming into fantasy, drive people's minds and emotions away from reality, leading to bold escapes from what is real, thus causing considerable damage to the process of inner maturation.

Apparently outdated, myths have lost their power of expression but not their content, because they are imbedded in the history of evolution of human beings themselves.

Let's keep in mind that as old *fairytales* such as *Little Red Riding Hood*, and similar ones, were sidelined by educational programs, industrialization and the human struggle to consume it produced a terrible existential vacuum, robbing human life of its deep meaning.

Given the absence of an appropriate psychological language to fill these gaps during the physical life, new *gods* have been created in keeping with the behavioral parameters of the day, masking many conflicts and calling on old myths to overhaul the being's *disinteresting* and tiresome operational journey.

So loud and primitive music made a comeback, requiring tribal moves infused with exacerbated sensuality, encouraging the practice of irresponsible sex and the intoxication of the senses, as sources of pleasure and abysses when one can forget about the responsibilities of the conscience in the face of intellectual and moral evolutionary demands.

Sports resuscitated their gladiators –in the most violent ones– or brought back the demigods in competitions of all kinds, always striving to win, with no regard for the joy of competition.

Merciless professionalism has disseminated organizations –some of them criminal, no doubt– where athletes are but mere commodities that get discarded when they are no longer useful to the interests of the mafia and the adoring fans –who, in turn, once willing to kill and to die for their idols, devour them, nonetheless, in the end...

Inflamed passions make the masses delirious, as myths rule over these events –some of which are violent, others barbaric, and a number of them downright ridiculous– made up almost entirely of puppets controlled by experts in the art of manipulation.

In these situations, gratification is substituted for the pleasure of the senses, which burns fast leaving people always desperate for more, given that this type of satisfaction does not offer beauty, tranquility, or harmony.

With the predominance of violent myths responsible for keeping primitive instincts alive –something humans should have overcome by now– said madness festivals drive the delirious masses to excess, to disastrous forms of entertainment whose consequences are fueled by drugs, by the exhaustion of the senses, by homicidal violence, and by the disintegration of the human identity...

At present, such mythological irruption is so cruel that many aficionados –overtaken by the avalanche of information put out by the reckless media– internalize the myths of power, glory, and physical strength. Building muscle and developing certain behaviors, they start believing they are predestined to physical immortality. They become fascinated by the idea of dragging around vast crowds of adoring fans, making their own existence unbearable. At this point, they can only go on by relying on drugs, which ruin them and lead them to death by *overdose.*

Initially, a desire for popularity pushes everyone over the abyss and any means of attracting attention –through an abominable, funny, unique, or an exotic appearance– creates a stereotype that fascinates people devoid of good sense, always searching for novelties. Once they gain notoriety, they surround themselves with security and wear disguises to keep the privacy they never had. They fear being found out and having their weaknesses and conflicts made public –otherwise only known by their entourage.

Human beings, however, continue to advance toward Reality, in which they are immersed –whether they like it or not– for every human is a living and inextinguishable spark.

Slowly —for progress is unstoppable— the momentarily menacing wave will come and go, followed by another one meant to also come and go. Evolution is simply inevitable and the search for the *Self* will enable a different behavior, making way for authenticity, the journey within, and self-discovery.

For still a long time to come, the prevalence of myth in the human unconscious will command its behavior. Despite its presence, programs for ascension will appear through dreams of beauty, peace, and complete freedom, which, in turn, will produce future archetypes that will become etched in the unconscious, since they proceed from the spirit world where life abounds. They will appear on the earth where these evolutionary programs will develop.

24

A BRIEF ESSAY ON EVIL

Good is everything that is in harmony with God's law, whereas evil is everything that deviates from it.
(The Spirits' Book – Question 630)

A tendency toward evil persists in the human spirit as a reminiscence of the ancestral primitivism inherent to the early stages of evolution.

Plato, in his profound observations, noticed it and called it the *dark side* of beings and, therefore, unknown and Carl Gustav Jung confirmed it in his studies about the personality, calling it the *shadow.*

That is where violent impulses, aggression, enslaving passions, and ungoverned instincts linger, answering for the delay in achieving self-illumination.

It is the *lower self,* which poses a danger to the individual. It must be identified and combated with the light of discernment and love.

It is almost always seen in other people as diseases of the soul, responsible for the unquestionable harm done to other individuals in particular or to society in general.

The more it remains unknown in our inner world the more harm and disturbances it causes.

The Spirit is not evil, given its divine origin. However, evil persists in it the same way debris clings to the precious stone, or chaff gets mixed in with the good wheat.

To ignore it is to let it run free and proliferate, allowing it to make frequent and harmful appearances in our behavior.

Likewise, any attempt to smother it with rigid attitudes is pointless, for the less it can express itself the stronger it becomes, until the time it explodes with untold force.

When a force under pressure encounters resistance, it continues to expand. Eventually, it either explodes or finds release.

In said cases, the right approach leads to its identification –the impulse– and to our capacity for resistance.

Along the anthropological process, the strongest biotype survived because of its brutality, size, and astuteness in the struggle for life.

As humans developed intelligence and applied it to protect themselves and preserve the species, they acquired the power to defeat beasts and gigantic animals. Consequently, the presence of evil remained predominant in them, which they have been using against themselves in the form of self-destruction, excess, vice, and against others in the form of theft, slander, persecution, killing, and wars that threaten our civilization at large.

To become aware of the presence of evil within ourselves we must engage in self-examination, finding the vulnerable areas that trigger it, predisposing us toward aggression.

Everyone is vulnerable to afflictions derived from illness, stress, aggression, and psychological disturbances.

During infancy, said emotions appear in the form of chaotic movements, crying, reflecting the child's feelings of helplessness in the face of pain, discomfort or some biological need.

Later on, the child bites to express fear or anger. After acquiring greater mobility, he or she slams on objects, hits, runs away, or plans revenge.

Depending on the child's environment, family life, and particularly the mother –with whom the child spends a greater amount of time– the evilness inherent to infancy either develops and grows or dramatically dissipates.

In adulthood, due to the presence of other feelings such as shame and guilt –which generate tension– fear and anger intensify, encouraging the practice of evil as a form of revenge or a cruel way to survive.

Evil can be considered an emergency emotion that erupts with violence when in fear or remains in silence, acting in the dark and perturbing the person who feels its constriction.

When evil manifests, it stimulates the sympathoadrenal system, which supplies the energy for the nefarious action –fight– or flight, until a favorable circumstance appears to release the tension.

As this force increases without release, fear transforms into anger, which escalates into fury and can sometimes lead to panic.

Humans fear pain.

Anything leading to pain, if the individual does not have fear under control by the truth and does not dominate their anger, exteriorizes in evil to attack and relax.

The will is pretty powerless in the face of fear, which irrupts with or without logical motive and frightens; however, it has a lot of power over anger, which can be managed.

Anger cannot be considered a destructive manifestation, but an organic reaction because it disappears once the causes go away.

When individuals feel trapped, the evil existing in them turns into a fury capable of breaking and destroying everything.

Fury blinds, obliterating reason and rendering the will powerless.

Guilt always irrupts after behavior that makes other people suffer, intentionally or not.

Initially, it is a feeling of shame regarding our own inferiority, which grows and transforms.

The onset of guilt gives us a sense of having lost the respect that inspired affection, generating misgivings and instability.

Shame in connection with our actions generates feelings of humiliation and rejection, pushing us toward emotional discomfort and unwarranted suspicions in an ongoing and bewildering mental battle.

When individuals are psychologically mature, they realize what happened and look for ways to make amends. However, when they are emotionally immature, they run away in shame and look for a mechanism to justify and punish themselves, something that triggers the dormant evil, which then transforms into resentment against self or the party that caused the situation.

The absence of responsibility causes individuals to blame other people for having created the circumstances that created the incident, even if such circumstances do not exist. It is a childish way for the person at fault to self-justify.

The predominating conflict does not allow individuals to discern clearly, so they always place the blame on others, hardly ever accepting personal responsibility.

The day comes, however, when evil sets the conscience free and a rational perception corrects the way in which the person understands the facts. At this point, the individual feels the need to make amends.

Likewise, when individuals feel insecure and fearful, the harmful action becomes a self-punishing mechanism, disturbing their psychological behavior.

Shame and guilt must be dealt with spontaneously and assertively the moment individuals accept that they are human, and therefore susceptible to episodes of bad judgment and to making mistakes, which can and must be corrected.

The discovery of the evil within –disguised as a variety of sentiments– contributes to its eradication, thereby investing in our emotional, spiritual, and behavioral health.

This is neither an easy nor a quick endeavor.

The elimination of negative conditioning happens when we strive to replace it with another, in this case, a healthy and beneficial one.

Any available space quickly fills up or remains vulnerable to being occupied, once again, by the old habit.

To each negative impulse produced by the evil lingering within us, we must apply a rational and serene formulation, thereby transforming a dangerous and vile reaction into a dignified and patient action.

The personality remains a still unexplored abyss with complex *mysteries* to unveil.

Millennia lie dormant in the being's unconscious. It is there that we find the automatic impulses that reason has been overcoming. Yet, they still require decoding in order to be diluted, giving way to uplifting action.

Inheriting past experiences, humans have affixed them to their conscience, which, in a way, begins to guide human behavior along the arduous path to self-consciousness, when individuals will know how to act with balance, respect *God's Laws,* and do everything according to God's will.

Undoubtedly, evil is the absence of good –yet to take up residency. Therefore, it contributes to assault and perturb life, even attempting to destroy it.

Its existence is real, continuing to afflict and generate pain, ultimately leading the person to undergo a radical behavioral change.

To deny its *reality* is a dangerous way to hide it.

This quality of the *inferior self* must give way to the totality of the Higher Self.

Thusly, evil is an automatic, unconscious impulse emerging from the being's *abyss* as a survival mechanism that unleashes disturbing, lingering tendencies.

Residing at the core, such tendencies are psychogenic; they are not produced by external factors, whatever their stimuli may be. Said stimuli will only be accepted on account of resonance –through attunement– with the vibrational wave synchronizing them.

Many perverted and vulgar images put out by the media perturb some individuals while they have no effect on others.

However, when the latent impulse of evil exists, external factors awaken it or vitalize it, if it was already in circulation.

Love plays an essential role in the therapy to dilute evil because it provides security to those who become victims of the imbalance produced by instinct, helping them to educate their will; adjust the lens through which they see life; and make gradual headway in the practice of the good –provided that this change is not sudden or induced by the enchantment of momentary enthusiasm.

Mental exercises in connection with uplifting thoughts and reflection about the life of selfless individuals help create a positive mental landscape where individuals can experience well-being without being prodded by envy, selfishness, or aggression.

Examining our actions and watching our behavior equally create the conditions for the liberating effect of prayer therapy, which elevates and envelops the Spirit in vibrations of a higher order that pervade it and frees it from evil, so that it may focus on the good, *according to God's Law.*

25
THE ENDLESS QUEST

Presumptuous ignorance answers for the innumerable evils that afflict human beings. Not just the ignorance derived from a lack of instruction, but mainly the kind that pretends to know what it does not; the kind that appears to know all things from a few bits of information.

Arrogant pseudo-intellectuals are as dangerous to social relations as are individuals learning at the most basic level, that is, individuals who genuinely ignore the subjects presented to them. Devoid of pretense, the latter are open to knowledge and, even more than learning, they become aware of how much they still need to learn, predisposing themselves to the task. Conversely, arrogant pseudo-intellectuals —believing to be in possession of the truth and filtering everything through the defective equipment they are so proud of— ruin many a blooming of hope and love, only because they do not seem compatible with their criteria to understand the world and broaden its horizons.

Petty in their groundless vanity, they charge with false superiority against everything that hurts their susceptibility, especially in connection with subjects they ignore —and lack the wisdom to admit it— trying to come across as being proficient in every field.

In their egocentric mindset, they think the world will have a hard time after their transient vessel of flesh passes.

Defenders of their own ideas, they deceive, stating to be at the service of humanity's freedom and cultural ideals. So, they avoid living on principle and become inveterate talkers, self-attributing the duty to save naïve individuals from equally astute individuals.

Since early on, intelligent humans on the earth understand how much they need to grow and humbly develop in relation to the cosmos. They study and experiment nonstop, respecting everyone's resources and increasingly endeavoring to acquire new knowledge as often as the opportunity arises.

They neither attack nor are they obstinate, remaining open to any and all kind of information, for they recognize that, despite having a great deal of knowledge in certain subjects, there are others they know nothing about.

As for spiritual matters, an immense territory unfolds filled with fascinating landscapes waiting to be conquered, bearing in mind that no one in the world is apt to set definitive concepts and paradigms for this is not within their realm of possibility.

However prolific and complex, human language is insufficient to describe reality's causes; it merely observes its effects.

The poverty of the language does not provide the elements –some vibrant and others delicate– to decode the marvelous impressions perceived by the limited physical senses.

How do we speak about unknown matters with unsuitable terms? How do we define emotions that we have not yet experienced with incorrect words? How do we explain what is *immaterial* with words associated to symbols we already know? How do we decipher thoughts without the brain, when the brain is incapable of explaining itself and still remains a mystery even to reason? How do we set physical parameters in an ocean of psychical, intelligent, and infinite energy? Would it be possible to establish behavioral guidelines for mediumistic phenomena when each individual constitutes a special equipment with its own characteristics? Why should we think that a personal conclusion, resulting from someone's studies and observations, should become the permanent, irrefutable parameter for all?

These are but a few of many questions we must reflect upon gradually. They show how many limitations still prevent us from issuing correct definitions about life itself, and the phenomena it generates along the Spirit's evolutionary path.

With great appropriateness, Allan Kardec analyzed the opinion of many inhabitants of the causal world, but left several questions open for the future, for he understood that he was saying n*either the first nor the last* word concerning this unique and vast symphony that life is.

Slightly opening the curtain that veiled the *invisible world,* he offered a partial view of that reality, benefiting humans with precious resources by way of mediumship to amplify it, thus increasing their capacity to understand and experience, which continues even after the death of the body.

Naturally, the fact that someone is discarnate does not mean that he or she has acquired absolute knowledge and can provide solid answers on any subject, or be the exclusive bearer of a revelation that would be as bombastic as it would be bogus.

When Allan Kardec adopted the *universal* approach for the teachings, he demonstrated his characteristic humility as well as the great deal of carefulness he applied to deal with the principles of immortality, communicability, and the spirit life. He did not go beyond the limitations imposed by the times and the culture, so that the information would appear according to the peoples' capacity for understanding. Likewise, the revelations arrived only when science was ready to put them to the test through research, and when the minds were prepared to understand them.

Nonetheless, individuals with pseudo-wisdom multiply in every sector of spiritual knowledge, from where they attack —armed with their arrogant ignorance— everything that strikes them as unproven, or lying outside the scope of knowledge that should remain stagnant in its cultural limitations, instead of following an ongoing process of research and development.

What today seems odd or unusual can later become accepted, professed to, and real.

We certainly cannot and should not abdicate good sense, logic, or reason which analyzes and reaches conclusions. Furthermore, we should clearly avoid closing ourselves off as if we were the only ones in possession of the truth.

The inevitable march of progress is awe-inspiring, and no one should consent to being left out of this unstoppable evolutionary mechanism.

The horizons of knowledge expand with each passing minute. Cultural and technological challenges multiply as do communications with Spirits whose mission is to provide moral, emotional, and psychical enrichment to individuals still living in a physical body.

Human beings move beyond what they already know to uncover new horizons and new worlds they intend to conquer, something they will accomplish through continuous effort.

In this quest for growth and glory, humility must be present from the start, for it grants greater access to the unlimited domains of the Infinite.

Arrogance is an obstacle on the road to spiritual growth, while simplicity of heart and a desire to learn are always a lever propelling forward and upward.

To be able to contemplate and reach the horizons of wisdom must be the goal of all those who side with love and the Good, aspiring to freedom and plenitude, while they still feel imprisoned in the narrow alleys of purifying reincarnations.

26
MORAL EDUCATION

Education has the critical task of transforming human beings, changing the moral landscape of society and planet Earth for the better.

Playing the essential role of firmly leading them through a systematic combat against ignorance, it becomes a moderating agent against aggression and the primitive passions, substituting them with healthy behavior which in turn develops noble sentiments, and instills an attitude of respect for life and its manifestations.

Thanks to its continuous action, codes of conduct are reformulated and experience a significant ethical transformation, thereby producing well-being, harmony, lofty aspirations, and higher achievements.

Broadening the horizons of human thought, education molds the human character at a higher level, efficiently enabling a healthy coexistence within the social group without stressful frictions or draining conflicts.

Education has the superior task of elevating humans to the summit of progress, presenting them with the infinite horizons waiting to be conquered and which are within their reach.

Its directives bring forth the beauty dormant within the coarse and brutish external form, unveiling the hidden angel needing to be released.

It speaks the language of harmony, but also that of sacrifice indispensable for the ascent.

However, this is not exclusively an academic, conventional education, but a moral education because it develops intelligence and emotion, habits and aspirations, and the integral being that lives forever.

A formal, systematic, memory-based and data gathering education contributes to improve technology and culture, which in turn develop external values and buying power for immediate consumption.

A moral education is geared to dealing with the ethical and behavioral challenges that shape human beings' internal structures enabling spiritual enrichment, through which they can calmly face the degenerative processes that consume the social organism.

It is a powerful antidote against violence and vulgarity, promoting individuals to better behavior, through which they preserve and develop the treasures of wisdom and honorable living.

Complementing formal instruction, moral education understands that beings come from evolutionary experiences that mark them with remnants and sequelae resulting from said past journeys, thus there is an impending need to instill teachings whose structures transcend the desire for pleasure and selfish pursuits –first as a humanistic principle and then as a humanitarian one.

Its postulates are slowly implemented and put down roots in direct proportion to the goals achieved.

Moral education lowers its probe into the spiritual reality to shape it, building the wings of angelhood without taking the feet off the ground all humans must tread.

Indeed, it is not about setting up philosophical or religious behavioral programs dictated by partisans of specific ideologies. It is about transmitting universal guidelines about duty, solidarity, love, understanding, citizenship rights, and, above and foremost, respect for everything and everyone, always working to achieve self-improvement and personal growth and, by extension, that of Humanity.

More than an elaborate and rigid rulebook geared toward the interests of specific groups, there is a need for a set of values suggesting the creation of organized groups capable of coexisting harmoniously with all other groups and social segments.

Moral education is not limited to buzzwords or outdated terms and anthologies. It is rather about peaceful and fraternal behavior encompassing all peoples and ways of life, in an immense embrace of dignity and admiration.

This moral contribution will give rise to individuals with moderate habits and rich in disciplined sentiments; individuals with healthy behavior that will propagate through the family, benefiting society as a whole.

Centered around the immortality of the soul, this educational work will propose the construction of the integral being, fostering the development of imperishable values relevant to the permanent reality, and not just to the transient physical personality in pursuit of goals that mean nothing after the grave.

In this complex landscape, the moral education of sentiments straighten them out proposing a program that instills increasingly improving behavior, as individuals go through the different phases of the evolutionary process.

When we can also provide powerful moral teachings —which encompass all the needs of the individual concerning self, others, and God– opportunities for growth increase, as do chances to be free from perturbing passions and pressing immediate needs devoid of real significance.

Through this valuable contribution –education of the sentiments– the heart grows tender, diluting the dominating atavistic brutality, opening the door to a whole host of spiritual achievements that multiply as individuals become more honorable.

Intellectual and artistic education, as well as professional experience, play an important role in the realization of human beings, but it is a moral education –the one not found in books, but in good examples– that will free them from negative conditionings and equip them with the necessary tools for their sublimation.

27
THE CHALLENGES POSED
BY AN IDEAL

When we are willing to fight for the implementation of any given ideal, we necessarily go through three specific phases indispensable for success: the dream, the plan, and the living of the ideal.

First, there must be something we consider as essential to our own existence. All lucid and noble individuals feel the need to promote humanity's progress as well as their own; it is a desire that springs from the unconscious and becomes a force capable of removing the most challenging of obstacles.

Like a dream, it begins to nourish the psyche that feeds off the delineation of the plan as it grows to occupy every available space within the mind and the heart. As much as we may try to take the ideal off our mind, it puts down roots and grows, becoming the basic reason for our existence.

It enraptures the individual in a very special kind of joy, lends musicality to the hours, and gives psychological meaning to the ascent.

Pouring forth from the Higher Spheres, it enriches the individual, as aspirations get delineated, eventually transforming into pure enchantment. Even the most severe challenges become fuel to continue with the struggles. None of the effort and sacrifice invested is seen as suffering. They serve as encouragement to reach the goal, which shines so bright in the psyche's inner landscape.

The dream is the decisive step in any project because it can be altered at every moment by changing shape, expanding, undergoing revision, and being readjusted countless times.

Such iridescent mind landscapes give a sense as to the infinite possibilities available to any and all individuals willing to do their part.

Like a *magic mirror* reflecting the metaphysical realities, it shows abstractions that one day will become objective phenomena in the realm of the human senses, which develop under their subtle commands.

A transcendental region, it is the delicate panel where humanity's mentors shape human aspirations, in which they chisel the thoughts that will create the future –foreseen through said aspirations– provided that there is silence to hear their unspoken voices.

Those who do not aspire; those who do not dream remain in the dreadful stages of the evolutionary process, unable to perceive the spiritual harmonies that envelop the Planet and all its inhabitants.

Passed that stage, and enraptured by the ideal, the person begins work on the planning phase.

Materializing an idea involves dealing with the difficulties to find the appropriate material and the right resources, identifying the most propitious circumstances and acquiring the necessary moral courage to avoid acting with haste, given that everything has its time.

Establishing higher ideals in the physical world implies encountering various natural obstacles on account of its dense structure, suitable to the preservation of ignorance and parasitism. When confronted with new projects that will alter the quality of human behavior, the status quo resists by erecting barriers.

Everything seems to conspire to make things difficult or to even downright obstruct change regarding what pleases the majority, which grants privilege to some at the expense of others as they cry and suffer and whose voices are not heard, deadened by the sound of vain celebrations where the deluded and the intoxicated try to drown their weaknesses...

No one, however, can stop the cyclonic force of progress or the march of evolution, which always erupt when least expected, cracking the foundation of deceitful power and causing its fall.

Stone by stone, in a continuous action, works of human and social ennoblement are erected to change lazy behavior —an accomplice of indifference— which, in turn, gives way to new impulses for remarkable achievements rendering life more appealing and making the human spirit unbeatable due to the force of its idealism.

In this all-out battle, martyrs emerge. Permanent victims appear so that brutal passions have a chance to hurt, and to satisfy those who are wrong concerning the reality of beings and their destiny. Nonetheless, those committed to changing the living conditions know that their example will fertilize other seeds, currently buried in the core of other heroes that will emerge in time.

After their passage and in their memory, many others will be encouraged to continue with the work that death does not interrupt. Often, they are the initial idealists themselves that return thanks to the blessing of reincarnation, to broaden society's possibilities to develop and change the sickly mentality that has dominated for so long.

The history of the establishment of ideals is a saga of sacrifice and abnegation on the part of those who became their honorable instruments.

In this context, painful situations do not breed discouragement. On the contrary, they further strengthen the idealists who feel projected into the future, which they can anticipate.

Slander, vilification, and the repercussion of unwarranted accusations give them even greater exposure than the dissemination of their excellent objectives. Anyone who has ever mobilized for the implementation of a noble ideal has suffered sordid and excruciating attacks at the hands of the adversaries of progress. Should said attacks fail to cause their defeat, adversaries resort to jokes and mockery trying to make them look ridiculous, incidentally generating exposure and eliciting respect in places where the idealists' voices were yet to be heard.

... And since their ideals were genuine, they found resonance amongst honest people, who free from ties with the interests of fools, joined in the effort to renew the social group in particular, and the world in general.

The next step is acceptance. The moment an ideal gains general recognition is crucial, for at this point the profound content of the idea becomes superficial and its expression is adulterated.

Basically, the stage of successful construction is a delicate one. It is at this stage that the selfishness of those who adhere manifests as they put forth personal suggestions that lie outside the context of the ideal, and unnecessary conflicts motivated by exhibitionism, vanity, and the exacerbation of the senses irrupt.

Idealists, however, having lived through the darkest hours, know the road they must now travel, so they skillfully proceed without being perturbed by momentary distractions, obstacles, and almost inevitable competitions.

Once the building phase has ended, maintenance programs and the phase of embodying the ideal require special care.

Now is the time to live the dream. There is no longer the need to run, be exhausted, overcome by despair, or insist despite impossible odds. Now is the time to start feeling the rewarding emotions resulting from the effort invested.

Not everyone can live a dream that has come true. The intense work pace, the ongoing exertion, and the endless nights have created such a habit of self-consuming frantic activity that a change in behavior seems impossible.

Despite their best intentions, idealists lose touch with reality and believe to be the *owners* of the work. Thinking no one can replace them, they become a source of conflict and compromised performance as they are unwilling to share, forgetting that we are all stewards of the Divine Concessions and will have to give an accounting of what has been done.

Indeed, living the dream is not staying away from the work. On the contrary, it is about living it in a different dimension; enjoying it in a different way; being happy for what has been achieved, thinking calmly about the countless budding possibilities, which other people may have to continue.

In so doing, peace fills the heart and trust —which never wavered— grows stronger and rejoices full of gratitude to the Source of Life, whence all things come.

Any ideal concerning the earth may be compared to beloved children conceived in love, for whose arrival every detail is tenderly and carefully planned and whose education receives our best efforts until is time to hand them over to their destiny for the continuation of their growth and that of Humanity.

Curtailing their development with our overprotection is to repress them and to deny society of one of its dear members due to an irrational and illogical desire to claim a tormenting proprietorship over life.

Just as parents are co-creators, laborers are co-builders whose performance is crowned with success once the part assigned to them is finished.

To dream about ideals conducive to human enrichment, to be committed to establishing said ideals, and to live the dream with love and gratefulness to God are giant steps that all individuals must promote in favor of themselves and society.

28
SOWING AND REAPING

When you see someone who is ill, consider the blessing of good health that you enjoy and reflect deeply upon your present existence.

You often react, losing your composure over small stuff that bothers you, such as an indiscreet friend spreading rumors about you; an unstable person maligning you; an incident at home, which could have been avoided; becoming irritated over unimportant events; criticism from someone who is close to you; pseudo loneliness; deceptive dissatisfaction. In short, countless situations that only affect you because you let them.

The enormous number of gifts that enrich your life, making it valuable and appealing, do not receive due consideration while nonsense darkens your days.

This is a profoundly ungrateful and perturbing attitude on your part concerning the assistance you receive from the Divine Mercy.

Despite their difficult circumstances, infirm brothers and sisters have not been abandoned by Providence either.

You should compare your situation with that of your fellow travelers currently affected by the consequences of their past actions —from which they cannot escape— while you are in a comfortable position to repeat experiences, rectify delusions, and make amends.

So, invigorate your spirit with courage and reconsider what needlessly mortifies you, taking advantage of the treasures in your possession in order to increase them and invest them in your benefit and that of others.

A physical rebirth is an educational opportunity for the Spirit to grow, self-illuminate, and improve at every moment. Since time passes very easily and very fast, there is no better alternative than to use it wisely and justly, reaping the best results possible.

✳

Infirm people confined to bodies that became cruel prisons with limited movement, notice the improper use they made of the limbs that carried them down the path of crime.

Those individuals you see suffering from congenital anomalies have also abused the resources of health and beauty, falling into an abyss of shadows through the false door of suicide, thus momentarily frustrating all the plans that were made for their evolution.

Men and women wandering in the mental shadows of aggressive insanity or locked in endless silence, revisit the violence perpetrated against other lives; the shameful treasons to which they consented; and the dark incursions into human rights' violations.

The mentally impaired you see laughing continuously, making bizarre facial expressions and suffering from tormenting convulsions have in turn deceived and betrayed someone's trust, whose feelings were destroyed and whose madness and deep-bleeding wounds now attach to the delicate areas of the perpetrator's psyche, causing a terrible spirit obsession.

Individuals writhing in excruciating pain and taking invisible stabbings reap the moral harvest of abominable acts committed against others when, from the illusory heights of power, they persecuted and caused merciless devastation.

It pains you to see the empty expression of an autistic person who suddenly turns aggressive; the profound sadness in the face of psychotic individuals who walk around in a somber mood, hating themselves as well as everything and everyone around them; the jerky body movements of somebody suffering from a neurological disorder that offers no respite to the despair of the patient and the caretakers; the mask of hatred in schizophrenics with homicidal or depraved tendencies; the vulgar and promiscuous behavior of people confined to filthy beds or to narrow and repugnant cells. They are, nonetheless, our brothers and sisters in agony undergoing severe correction to learn to respect moral principles and the human being, while simultaneously experiencing horrific spirit obsessions in an endless struggle with those they have harmed and whose feelings they have crushed.

Many others, crucified by degenerative diseases or indescribable moral afflictions cannot outrun their guilt or the Cosmic Consciousness, which commands life everywhere with equanimity.

They cannot escape the Sovereign Codes any more than you can.

The nature of an action determines the nature of the reaction.

While you are in possession of the healthy instruments of the physical body —which serves you as a vehicle for progress— walk decisively along the path of the Good, improving nonstop.

Do not let indolence, dissatisfaction, or apparent failure freeze the mechanisms of progress available to you.

Appreciate the gift of the passing hours and illumine yourself.

Often, success is the result of many sacrifices and imperfections. People unwilling to repeat the experience to get it right have lost the battle before it started.

Health, physical harmony, a good family, a lucid mind, honest work, and a few comforts ahead are also divine loans that you must use wisely so as not to return empty-handed and indebted, resorting to justifications that will not find resonance with the Laws governing your destiny.

On a closing note, remember Jesus, who at all times used the sublime resources at His disposal to love and serve, pointing in the direction of happiness that begins with the momentous decision to self-illuminate.

29
LETTING GO

Surrender is the great adversary of arrogance —selfishness and pride's favorite child.

When individuals can break the expertly forged chains that hold them captive in the prison without of the primitive passions —where they have been caught in the vicious circle of deceiving pleasure— they can face themselves and discover the sickly whims of the *ego* along with all the disguises it uses to remain dominant.

As individuals sift through their deepest emotions, they perceive that many of the factors that justify the unsound behavior they display in social circles are plotted by that prominent figure of egotism, which seeks to dominate in every situation, thus giving rise to pride – the unhappy matrix of reprehensible discrimination and criminal behavior.

Selfishness and pride are the womb for the pestilence that leads people to behave arrogantly on account of a false superiority, to demand special privileges for themselves, and to impose their morbid whims.

Humility, on the other hand —that paramount evolutionary achievement— giving a real dimension as to the value of human beings before the cosmos, is the silent and serene combatant that gradually takes possession of the different areas of the emotions, for it verifies the ephemeral nature of vanity and the absence of an emotional and human legitimate purpose.

Humble individuals right away let go of all things devoid of real value, since they are the product of illusion: nobility titles; community awards for honor, courage, volunteer work, beauty, cultural achievement, or artistic talent, because as circumstances change, or as people paying honors are replaced by individuals who think differently, awards might be taken away. Additionally, disease and moral weaknesses may change the behavior of the honorees. Should they give in to pride, they would become objectionable or demented, aggressive or extravagant, snobbish or perverse.

While in the physical body, Spirits are always subject to many vicissitudes, requiring constant vigilance and frequent prayer to get rid of their own pettiness in the form of perturbing passions.

Individuals must let go of all that is superfluous.

They accumulate useless things in the hopes of using them one day –which never comes.

They gather objects to which they attribute meaning – despite the fact that they remain soulless– when what they really need in their loneliness is company.

They fight over land and fields, which they appropriate, engaging in terrible abuses to maintain them, fomenting misery among the dispossessed, and fighting homeless invaders, while they have not the slightest need of all they have.

They greedily hold on to shoes, accessories and jewelry that clog up entire closets and drawers, which, at any rate, can only be worn one at a time. Over time, the inventory grows as a result of ever-changing fashion.

They collect cars –in inconceivable usury– only to drive each vehicle every now and then.

Bank accounts lay dead in fluctuating investments when they would produce returns if used in beneficent work and humanitarian causes, generating jobs that confer dignity to human beings and resolving –or at least minimizing– the problem of hunger and the world's endemic diseases, thereby completely changing the current human geopolitics.

The frenzy to acquire electronic[16] devises overwhelms people leading them to excess with hardly a chance to install them or time to enjoy them…

… But exorbitant pride intensifies people's greed and drives them to show off and discuss their ephemeral conquests.

What is essential is more important than what is superfluous, which never has any usefulness for their keepers.

In the insanity that prevails in frantic shopping and high-end living, it is difficult to distinguish between what is valuable and what merely appears to be.

Freedom and, by extension, happiness, only emerge once we learn the art of letting go.

Share your surplus –what you do not need– with those who need it, improving other lives.

Value your time by simplifying your existence, decreasing the number of useless objects and complexities.

As you let go of things that generate affliction over the burden of possession and the fear of loss, emotional space emerges, which you can fill with aspirations that time does not consume, thieves do not steal, and moths cannot destroy.

---

16. This book was dictated in 1999. – Tr.

Psychical space currently taken up by pointless immediate whims will give way to the installation of healing reflections, restorative experiences, and lasting peace.

As you let go of external objects, you will also let go of enslaving addictions, breaking away from painful constrictions imposed by pride and the ego, so that you may discover the beauty of love that expands and brings plenitude to your heart.

So, start to let go from this very moment of everything devoid of real value, and advance toward spiritually detachment from your earthly futilities.

Made in the USA
Middletown, DE
11 August 2022

71134351R00116